The American Novel seri̶e̶ _____ _____ _____ _____ ...terature with introductory critical guides to the great works of American literature. Each volume begins with a substantial introduction by a distinguished authori-ty on the text, giving details of the work's compo̶s̶i̶t̶i̶o̶n̶, publication histo-r̶y̶ a̶n̶d̶ c̶o̶n̶t̶e̶m̶porary reception, as well as ̶a̶ ̶g̶u̶i̶d̶e̶ ̶t̶o̶ ̶i̶t̶s̶ ̶l̶a̶t̶e̶r̶ critical t̶r̶e̶n̶ds and readings from first publication to ̶t̶h̶e̶ ̶p̶r̶e̶s̶e̶n̶t̶ ̶d̶a̶y̶. ̶T̶h̶i̶s̶ is followed by a group of new essays, each specially commissioned from a leading scholar in the field, which together constitute a forum of inter-pretative methods and prominent contemporary ideas on the text. There are also helpful guides to further reading. Specifically designed for under-graduates, the series will be a powerful resource for anyone engaged in the critical analysis of major American novels and other important texts.

★ The American Novel ★

GENERAL EDITOR

Emory Elliott
University of California, Riverside

New Essays on
Song of Solomon

Edited by
Valerie Smith

CAMBRIDGE
UNIVERSITY PRESS

Published by the Press Syndicate of the University of Cambridge
The Pitt Building, Trumpington Street, Cambridge CB2 1RP
40 West 20th Street, New York, NY 10011-4211, USA
10 Stamford Road, Oakleigh, Melbourne 3166, Australia

First published 1995

Printed in the United States of America

Library of Congress Cataloging-in-Publication Data
New essays on Song of Solomon / edited by Valerie Smith.
p.   cm. – (The American novel)
Includes bibliographical references.
ISBN 0-521-45440-9 – ISBN 0-521-45604-5 (pbk.)
1. Morrison, Toni. Song of Solomon. 2. Afro-American families in
literature. 3. Afro-Americans in literature. 4. Michigan – In
literature. I. Smith, Valerie, 1956– . II. Series.
PS3563.08749S636   1994
813'.54 – dc20
94-7334

A catalog record for this book is available from the British Library.

ISBN 0-521-45440-9 hardback
ISBN 0-521-45604-5 paperback

Contents

v

Contents

5

The Postmodernist Rag:
Political Identity and the Vernacular
in *Song of Solomon*
WAHNEEMA LUBIANO
page 93

Series Editor's Preface

In literary criticism the last twenty-five years have been particularly fruitful. Since the rise of the New Criticism in the 1950s, which focused attention of critics and readers upon the text itself – apart from history, biography, and society – there has emerged a wide variety of critical methods which have brought to literary works a rich diversity of perspectives: social, historical, political, psychological, economic, ideological, and philosophical. While attention to the text itself, as taught by the New Critics, remains at the core of contemporary interpretation, the widely shared assumption that works of art generate many different kinds of interpretation has opened up possibilities for new readings and new meanings.

Before this critical revolution, many American novels had come to be taken for granted by earlier generations of readers as having an established set of recognized interpretations. There was a sense among many students that the canon was established and that the larger thematic and interpretative issues had been decided. The task of the new reader was to examine the ways in which elements such as structure, style, and imagery contributed to each novel's acknowledged purpose. But recent criticism has brought these old assumptions into question and has thereby generated a wide variety of original, and often quite surprising, interpretations of the classics, as well as of rediscovered novels such as Kate Chopin's *The Awakening*, which has only recently entered the canon of works that scholars and critics study and that teachers assign their students.

The aim of The American Novel series is to provide students of American literature and culture with introductory critical guides to

American novels now widely read and studied. Each volume is devoted to a single novel and begins with an introduction by the volume editor, a distinguished authority on the text. The introduction presents details of the novel's composition, publication history, and contemporary reception, as well as a survey of the major critical trends and readings from first publication to the present. This overview is followed by four or five original essays, specifically commissioned from senior scholars of established reputation and from outstanding younger critics. Each essay presents a distinct point of view, and together they constitute a forum of interpretative methods and of the best contemporary ideas on each text.

It is our hope that these volumes will convey the vitality of current critical work in American literature, generate new insights and excitement for students of the American novel, and inspire new respect for and new perspectives upon these major literary texts.

Emory Elliott
University of California, Riverside

1

Introduction

VALERIE SMITH

1

A FRICAN American cultural workers – writers, artists, film-
makers, etc. – are often granted the dubious accolade of "universal" or "more than black." Such designations are meant to
suggest that their accomplishments appeal to an audience larger
than the African American community. Unfortunately, they suggest as well that the category of "the universal" transcends the
particularities and contingencies of cultural specificity and that
racial specificity is less desirable than putative universality.

Recent debates about the literary canon (the body of works
historically and commonly considered great) have held the notion
of universality up to heightened scrutiny. Defenders of the traditional canon typically argue that texts historically judged as great
meet timeless artistic criteria, standards that transcend constructions of race, gender or ethnicity. When challenged to defend the
practice of largely excluding literature written by people of color
and by white women, they accuse revisionists of confusing politics
or demographics with literary standards. Those who would en-
shrine U.S. literary history as it has commonly been written thus
deny that the predominance of white male writers bespeaks a set
of class or political interests.

In contrast, critics who seek to expand the canon of U.S. letters
are likely to argue that all literary judgments are ideologically
grounded; by this light, the denial of political interests reflects a
desire to maintain the status quo. They posit as well that it is in the
very nature of power to obscure its own agency and contingencies.
Traditionalists thus would accuse works by African American writers, for instance, of being about race while works by white writers

1

are not. Likewise, they would argue that works by women are about gender while texts by men are not. Revisionists would respond that that logic works only if one assumes that blackness is a racial category while whiteness is not, or that womanhood is a gender issue while manhood is not.

Toni Morrison ranks among the most highly regarded and widely read fiction writers and cultural critics in the history of U.S. literature. Novelist, editor, playwright, and essayist, Morrison enjoys such high regard and general esteem both in this country and internationally that she invites frequent comparison with the best-known writers of the American and European literary canons: William Faulkner, James Joyce, Thomas Hardy, and others. Indeed, certain critics would seek to compliment Morrison by describing her as something more than an African American, or woman, or black woman writer.

However, Morrison is a leading voice in current debates about constructions of race and gender in U.S. literature and culture. As a critic of both her own fiction and the work of other writers, she refuses to allow race to be relegated to the margins of literary discourse. Moreover, throughout her fiction she uses narrative forms both to express the nuances of African American oral and musical culture and to reclaim black historical experience.

In an interview with Nellie McKay, Morrison explains her reluctance to being compared primarily with classic white authors:

> I am not *like* James Joyce; I am not *like* Thomas Hardy; I am not *like* Faulkner. I am not *like* in that sense. I do not have objections to being compared to such extraordinarily gifted and facile writers, but it does leave me sort of hanging there when I know that my effort is to be *like* something that has probably only been fully expressed in music, or in some other culture-gen that survives almost in isolation because the community manages to hold on to it.[1]

Morrison expands upon this position in a profoundly persuasive and influential essay entitled "Unspeakable Things Unspoken: The Afro-American Presence in American Literature." Here she explores the significance of the silence surrounding the topic of race in the construction of American literary history.

Morrison begins the essay by questioning the idea of a canon and interrogating the presupposition of whiteness that the American canon inscribes. The fact that certain critics continue to deny that black writers are excluded from the U.S. literary canon on the basis of race, she argues, demonstrates that race remains an unspeakable topic in American culture.

> For three hundred years black Americans insisted that "race" was no usefully distinguishing factor in human relationships. During those same three centuries every academic discipline, including theology, history, and natural science, insisted "race" was *the* determining factor in human development. When blacks discovered they had shaped or become a culturally formed race, and that it had specific and revered difference, suddenly they were told there is no such thing as "race," biological or cultural, that matters and that genuinely intellectual exchange cannot accommodate it.[2]

To her mind, the custodians of the canon retreat into specious arguments about quality and the irrelevance of ideology when defending the critical status quo against charges of being exclusionary. Morrison is, in addition, skeptical about arguments based on the notion of critical quality, since the term is so frequently self-justifying and contested.

She then considers the ways that recent approaches to African American literary study respond to critical attempts to delegitimate black literary traditions. While some critics deny that African American art exists, Afro-Americanists have rediscovered texts that have long been suppressed or ignored, have sought to make places for African American writing within the canon, and have developed ways of interpreting these works. There are also critics who would argue that African American art is inferior – "imitative, excessive, sensational, mimetic . . . , and unintellectual, though very often 'moving,' 'passionate,' 'naturalistic,' 'realistic' or sociologically 'revealing.'"[3] Those critics, Morrison notes, often lack the acumen or commitment to understand the works' complexity. In response to such labels, Afro-Americanists have devised such strategies as applying recent literary theories to black literature so that these noncanonical texts can participate in the formation of current critical discourse and debate.

Morrison problematizes most fully those who seek to ennoble African American art by measuring it in relation to the ostensibly universal criteria of Western art. She remarks that such comparisons fail to do justice both to the indigenous qualities of the texts and to the traditions of which they are a part.

Morrison describes three subversive strategies that critics can utilize in order to undermine these attempts to marginalize African American art and literature. To counteract such assaults, she first proposes that critics develop a theory of literature that responds to the tradition's indigenous qualities: "one that is based on its culture, its history, and the artistic strategies the works employ to negotiate the world it inhabits."[4] Second, she suggests that the canon of classic, nineteenth-century literature be reexamined to reveal the ways in which the African American cultural presence makes itself felt in these ostensibly white texts. Third, she recommends that contemporary mainstream and minority literary texts be studied for evidence of this presence.

Morrison's essay centers on the second and third strategies, because of her apparent fascination with the meanings that attach to the idea of absence:

> We can agree, I think, that invisible things are not necessarily "not-there"; that a void may be empty, but it is not a vacuum. In addition, certain absences are so stressed, so ornate, so planned, they call attention to themselves; arrest us with intentionality and purpose, like neighborhoods that are defined by the population held away from them. Looking at the scope of American literature, I can't help thinking that the question should never have been "Why am I, an Afro-American, absent from it?" It is not a particularly interesting query anyway. The spectacularly interesting question is "What intellectual feats had to be performed by the author or his critic to erase me from a society seething with my presence, and what effect has that performance had on the work?" What are the strategies of escape from knowledge? Of willful oblivion?[5]

Her incisive reading of Herman Melville's *Moby-Dick* as a critique of the power of whiteness exemplifies the second strategy she outlines and indicates the subtext of race that critics of that classic text have long ignored. She demonstrates the third strategy by discussing the opening sentences of each of her novels to suggest ways in which African American culture inscribes itself in black texts. Morrison's analyses of her own prose reverberate and shimmer. They display the acuity of her critical sensibility and her uses of language to reveal the subtleties of African American cultural life.

Morrison's critical study *Playing in the Dark: Whiteness and the Literary Imagination* expands upon the enterprise of "Unspeakable Things" and explores the impact of constructions of whiteness and blackness upon a range of key texts in the American literary tradition. To the extent that race has remained an almost unutterable subject in U.S. culture, her project is especially bold and necessary to our understanding of our national literature. As she writes:

> It has occurred to me that the very manner by which American literature distinguishes itself as a coherent entity exists because of this unsettled and unsettling population [Africans and African Americans]. Just as the formation of the nation necessitated coded language and purposeful restriction to deal with the racial disingenuousness and moral frailty at its heart, so too did the literature, whose founding characteristics extend into the twentieth century, reproduce the necessity for codes and restriction. Through significant and underscored omissions, startling contradictions, heavily nuanced conflicts, through the way writers peopled their work with the signs and bodies of this presence – one can see that a real or fabricated Africanist presence was crucial to their sense of Americanness.[6]

As part of the complex project of this work, Morrison establishes the discourses of race within which texts by Willa Cather, Melville, Edgar Allan Poe, Ernest Hemingway, and others participate. By making explicit the assumptions about race inscribed within the texts upon which she focuses, Morrison reveals the centrality of ideas of whiteness and blackness to the idea of America.

Morrison's commitment to representing and preserving the qualities of African American cultural life in her own prose and to identifying the impact of race in the work of others may be traced at least partly to the circumstances of her early life. She was born Chloe Anthony Wofford on February 18, 1931, in Lorain, Ohio, a multiracial steel town. From her parents and other relatives, she received a legacy of resistance to oppression and exploitation and an appreciation of African American folklore and cultural practices. Her maternal grandparents emigrated from Alabama to Ohio in hopes of leaving racism and poverty behind and finding greater opportunities for their children. Her father, likewise, left Georgia to escape the racial violence that was rampant there.

Morrison recalls the ubiquitousness of African American cultural rituals in her childhood and adolescence; the music, folklore, ghost stories, dreams, signs, and visitations that are so vividly evoked in her fiction have been shaping and empowering presences in her life as well.

The impact of these forces in her life has inspired her to capture the qualities of African American cultural expression in her prose. Indeed, Morrison and her critics alike have described the influence of orality, call and response, jazz, and dance in her narratives. Yet the presence of myth, enchantment, and folk practices in her work never offers an escape from the sociopolitical conditions that have shaped the lives of African Americans. Cultural dislocation, migration, and urbanization provide the inescapable contexts within which her explorations of the African American past are located.

In an essay entitled "Rootedness: The Ancestor as Foundation," Morrison describes the importance of orality and call and response in her fiction:

> [Literature] should try deliberately to make you stand up and make you feel something profoundly in the same way that a Black preacher requires his congregation to speak, to join him in the sermon . . . that is being delivered. In the same way that a musician's music is enhanced when there is a response from the audience. Now in a book, which closes, after all – it's of some importance to me to try to make that connection – to try to make that happen also. And, having at my disposal only the letters of the alphabet and some punctuation, I have to provide the places and spaces so that the reader can participate. Because it is the affective and participatory relationship between the artist or the speaker and the audience that is of primary importance, as it is in these other art forms I have described.[7]

Literature also played an important role in Morrison's childhood and youth. She was the only child in her first-grade class who was able to read when she entered school. As an adolescent she read widely across a variety of literary traditions, counting the classic Russian novelists, Flaubert, and Jane Austen among her favorites.

She was not exposed to the work of previous generations of black women writers until her adulthood. Her delayed introduction to the work of earlier black women writers does not, to her mind, mean that she writes outside that tradition. Rather, the connections between her work and theirs confirm her notion that African American women writers represent character and circumstance in specific, identifiable ways. As she remarks in a conversation with Gloria Naylor:

> [People] who are trying to show certain kinds of connections between myself and Zora Neale Hurston are always dismayed and disappointed in me because I hadn't read Zora Neale Hurston except for one little short story before I began to write. . . . [The] fact that I had never read Zora Neale Hurston and wrote *The Bluest Eye* and *Sula* anyway means that the tradition really exists. You know, if I had read her, then you could say that I consciously was following in the footsteps of her, but the fact that I never read her and still there may be whatever they're finding, similarities and dissimilarities, whatever such critics do, makes the cheese more binding, not less, because it means that the world as perceived by black women at certain times does exist[;] however they treat it and whatever they select out of it to record, there is that.[8]

Susan L. Blake quotes Morrison's remark that although the works she read in her youth "were not written for a little black girl in Lorain, Ohio . . . they spoke to [her] out of their own specificity." During those years Morrison had hopes of becoming a dancer; nevertheless, her early reading inspired her later "to capture that same specificity about the nature and feeling of the culture [she] grew up in."[9]

Morrison graduated with honors from Lorain High School and then attended Howard University, where she majored in English and minored in classics and from which she graduated in 1953. She describes the Howard years with some measure of ambivalence. Evidently, she was disappointed with the atmosphere at the university, which, she has said, "was about getting married, buying clothes and going to parties. It was also about being cool, loving Sarah Vaughan (who only moved her hand a little when she sang) and MJQ [the Modern Jazz Quartet]."[10] To offset the influence of these sorts of preoccupations, she became involved in the Howard University Players and traveled with a student–faculty repertory troupe that took plays on tour throughout the South during the summers. As Blake suggests, these trips illustrated for Morrison the stories of injustice her grandparents told about their lives in Alabama.

After graduation from Howard, Morrison received an M.A. from Cornell University in 1955, where she wrote a thesis on the theme of suicide in the works of William Faulkner and Virginia Woolf. She then taught at Texas Southern University from 1955 to 1957 and at Howard from 1957 to 1964. While at Howard she married Harold Morrison (from whom she is now divorced) and had two sons. During this period she also joined a writers' group, within which she wrote a story about a young black girl who wanted blue eyes. From that story eventually came *The Bluest Eye* (1970), her first novel.

After leaving Howard, Morrison returned to Lorain with her two young sons for an eighteen-month period. Subsequently, she began to work in publishing, first as an editor at L. W. Singer, the textbook subsidiary of Random House in Syracuse, New York, and then as senior editor at the headquarters of Random House in Manhattan. While she lived in Syracuse she worked on the manuscript of what was to become *The Bluest Eye* at night while her children slept. In her conversation with Gloria Naylor, she suggests that she resumed work on this novel almost as if to write herself back into existence:

> And so it looked as though the world was going by and I was not in that world. I used to live in this world, I mean really lived in it. I knew it. I used to really belong here. And at some point I didn't belong here anymore. I was somebody's parent, somebody's this, somebody's that, but there was no me in this world. And I was looking for that dead girl and I thought I might talk about that dead girl, if for no other reason than to have it, somewhere in the world, in a drawer. There was such a person. I had written this little story earlier just for some friends, so I took it out and I began to work it up. And all of those people were me. I was Pecola, Claudia . . . I was everybody. And as I began to do it, I began to pick up scraps of things I had seen or felt, or didn't see or didn't feel, but imagined.

And speculated about and wondered about. And I fell in love with myself. I reclaimed myself and the world – a real revelation. I named it. I described it. I listed it. I identified it. I recreated it.[11]

She sent part of a draft to an editor, who liked it enough to suggest that she finish it. *The Bluest Eye* was published by Holt, Rinehart, and Winston in 1970.

Although Morrison was not familiar with much writing by other African American writers when she began her first novel, she has had a profound impact upon the careers of a range of black authors. As senior editor at Random House, Morrison brought a number of black writers to that publisher's list, including Toni Cade Bambara, Angela Davis, Henry Dumas, and Gayl Jones. Gloria Naylor describes most eloquently the impact that Morrison's work had on her as a young author:

> The presence of [*The Bluest Eye*] served two vital purposes at that moment in my life. It said to a young poet, struggling to break into prose, that the barriers were flexible; at the core of it all is language, and if you're skilled enough with that, you can create your own genre. And it said to a young black woman, struggling to find a mirror of her worth in this society, not only is your story worth telling but it can be told in words so painstakingly eloquent that it becomes a song.[12]

From 1967 until 1988 Morrison taught at a number of colleges and universities, including Yale, Bard, the State University of New York at Purchase, and the State University of New York at Albany. Since 1988 she has held the Robert F. Goheen Professorship of the Humanities at Princeton University.

To date, Morrison has published six novels, each of which has enjoyed critical acclaim and sustained scholarly attention. In addition to *The Bluest Eye*, the list of her works includes *Sula* (1973) and *Song of Solomon* (1977), which received the National Book Critics' Circle Award in 1978 and was a Book-of-the-Month Club selection. *Tar Baby* (1981) was a bestseller and *Beloved* (1987) won the 1988 Pulitzer Prize for Fiction. *Jazz*, her most recent novel, was published in 1992.

Morrison is also a highly regarded essayist and has edited two collections of essays. In addition to *Jazz*, 1992 saw the publication of *Playing in the Dark: Whiteness and the Literary Imagination,* which is a collection of her own critical essays, and *Race-ing Justice, Engendering Power: Essays on Anita Hill, Clarence Thomas, and the Construction of Social Reality.* The appearance of three such diverse works in one year testifies both to Morrison's productivity and to her importance on the national intellectual scene. Few others are able to claim such distinction as novelist, literary critic, and cultural analyst.

In each of her novels, Morrison boldly undermines the assumptions and hierarchies that historically have legitimated the oppression of people of color, women, and the poor in U.S. culture. Her prose simultaneously invokes the lyrical and the historical, the supernatural and the ideological; she seeks to show the place of "enchantment" for people like the ones among whom she came of age, even as she explores the complex social circumstances within which they live out their lives. As she says in an interview with Christina Davis:

> My own use of enchantment simply comes because that's the way the world was for me and for the black people that I knew. In addition to the very shrewd, down-to-earth, efficient way in which they did things and survived things, there was this other knowledge or perception, always discredited but nevertheless there, which informed their sensibilities and clarified their activities. . . .
>
> I grew up in a house in which people talked about their dreams with the same authority that they talked about what "really" happened. They had visitations and did not find that fact shocking and they had some sweet, intimate connection with things that were not empirically verifiable. . . . Without that, I think I would have been quite bereft because I would have been dependent on so-called scientific data to explain hopelessly unscientific things and also I would have relied on information that even subsequent objectivity has proved to be fraudulent.[13]

2

Song of Solomon was enthusiastically received and widely reviewed. Its publication catapulted Morrison into the ranks of the most revered contemporary writers. In addition to the National Book Critics' Circle Award, she also received for it an American Academy and Institute of Arts and Letters Award. In 1980 President Jimmy Carter appointed her to the National Council on the Arts, and in 1981 she was elected to the American Academy and Institute of Arts and Letters.

Throughout the early to mid-1980s, *Song of Solomon* was the subject of much critical attention and ranked among the most frequently taught of Morrison's novels. Since its publication in 1987, *Beloved* has enjoyed exceptional popularity among general readers and scholars alike. And I suspect that given the profound ways in which *Jazz* meditates upon the nature of loss occasioned by the processes of migration and urbanization, that novel will also generate extensive debate. Although *Song of Solomon* may not be as popular as it was even a few years ago, it remains a key text in the corpus of Morrison's work and in the literary traditions of which it is a part. As the essays in this collection demonstrate, it is a work that powerfully explores the nature of family, identity, and culture within a society still burdened by the legacy of slavery and its aftermath of racial violence, and anticipates both thematically and stylistically Morrison's later fiction. The novel rewards scrutiny from a range of theoretical perspectives and is deeply rooted in the traditions that have shaped and inflected African American culture.

Song of Solomon tells the story of Milkman Dead's unwitting search for identity. Milkman appears to be destined for a life of self-alienation and isolation because of his commitment to the materialism and the linear conception of time that are part of the legacy he receives from his father, Macon Dead. However, during a trip to his ancestral home, Milkman comes to understand his place in a cultural and familial community and to appreciate the value of conceiving of time as a cyclical process.

The Deads exemplify the patriarchal, nuclear family that has traditionally been a stable and critical feature not only of American society but of Western civilization in general. The primary institution for the reproduction and maintenance of children, ideally it provides individuals with the means for understanding their place in the world. The degeneration of the Dead family and the destructiveness of Macon's rugged individualism symbolize the invalidity of American, indeed Western, values. Morrison's depiction of this family demonstrates the incompatibility of received assumptions with the texture and demands of life in black American communities.

Pilate Dead, Macon's younger sister, provides a marked contrast to her brother and his family. While Macon's love of property and money determines the nature and quality of his relationships, Pilate's sheer disregard for status, occupation, hygiene, and manners is accompanied by an ability to affirm spiritual values such as compassion, respect, loyalty, and generosity.

Pilate introduces a quality of "enchantment" into the novel. The circumstances of her birth make her a character of supernatural proportions. She delivered herself at birth and was born without a navel. Her smooth stomach isolates her from society. Moreover, her physical condition symbolizes her lack of dependence on others. Her self-sufficiency and isolation prevent her from being trapped or destroyed by the extremely decaying values that threaten her brother's life.

Before Milkman leaves his home in Michigan, he perceives the world in materialistic, unyielding terms that recall his father's behavior. Indeed, the search for gold that sends him to Virginia reveals his perception that escaping from his past and his responsibilities and finding material treasure will guarantee him a sense of his own identity.

Milkman's assumption that his trip south holds the key to his liberation is correct, although it is not gold that saves him. In his ancestors' world, communal and mythical values prevail over individualism and materialism; when he adopts their assumptions in place of his own, he arrives at a more complete understanding of what his experience means.

Milkman's development rests partly on his comprehending the ways in which his life is bound up with the experiences of others and partly on his establishing an intimate connection with the land for which his grandfather died. These accomplishments attend his greater achievement: learning to complete, understand, and sing the song that contains the history of his family. Milkman comes to know fully who he is when he can supply the lyrics to the song Pilate has only partially known. The song, which draws on African and African American stories of blacks who escaped slavery by flying back to Africa, explains Milkman's lifelong fascination with flight. When Milkman learns the whole song and can sing it to Pilate as she has sung it to others, he assumes his destiny. He understands his yearning toward flight as a way in which his ancestral past makes itself known and felt to him.

Milkman's sense of identity emerges when he allows himself to accept his personal and familial past. His quest critiques the faith in self-sufficiency for which his father stands. Through his story, Morrison questions Western conceptions of individualism and offers more fluid, destabilized constructions of identity.

This all-too-brief summary is meant to suggest some of the various polarities that Morrison juxtaposes in the novel: material pursuit and selflessness, history and myth, escape and commitment, past and present, and so on. Yet even as she explores terms which at first glance seem mutually exclusive, the world Morrison constructs here cannot be described neatly in terms of binary oppositions, a point several essays in this collection bring out. Rather, she examines the multiple connections and tensions that bind these ostensible oppositions within the lives of individuals and communities.

In "Unspeakable Things Unspoken," Morrison analyzes the first sentence of the novel. Her reading merits citing here because it displays how her subtle manipulation of language opens up some of the profound complexities of African American life that shape her characters' world.[14] The novel begins with the sentence "The North Carolina Mutual Life Insurance agent promised to fly from Mercy to the other side of Lake Superior at three o'clock." Seemingly straightforward, the sentence, as Morrison writes, mocks "a journalistic style." "Simple words, uncomplex sentence structures, persistent understatement, highly aural syntax – but the ordinariness of the language, its colloquial, vernacular, humorous and, upon occasion, parabolic quality sabotage expectations and mask judgments when it can no longer defer them."[15] Despite its superficial simplicity it anticipates many of the significant issues that the novel engages elsewhere.

For instance, the sentence takes the reader from North Carolina to Lake Superior. The geographical trajectory alludes to the process of northern migration that has been a defining moment both for the characters in the novel and for large numbers of African Americans in the twentieth century. The reference to "Lake Superior," as Morrison notes, is somewhat ironic, since the Promised Land of the North is also inevitably a place of disappointment.

Additionally, the references to flight and mercy direct our attention to two of the most significant motifs in the novel. Milkman is haunted by flight, perhaps because of the importance of flight to his ancestor Solomon and to other enslaved Africans as well. And even as references to flying resurface throughout the text, their meanings vary dramatically. Everyone fortunate enough to escape also abandons loved ones whose longings and sense of loss can never entirely be satisfied or consoled. As Morrison explains:

> So the agent's flight, like that of the Solomon in the title, although toward asylum (Canada, or freedom, or home, or the company of the welcoming dead), and although it carries the possibility of failure and the certainty of danger, is toward change, an alternative way, a cessation of things-as-they-are. It should not be understood as a simple desperate act, the end of a fruitless life, a life without gesture, without examination, but as obedience to a deeper contract with his people. It is his commitment to them, regardless of whether, in all its details, they understand it.[16]

The idea of mercy is likewise central to the novel, as Morrison remarks. Whatever the various characters believe themselves to be seeking, all are in search of mercy; only acts of mercy have the power to heal hurts both personal and cultural.

> It touches, turns and returns to Guitar at the end of the book – he who is least deserving of it – and moves him to make it his own final gift. It is what one wishes for Hagar; what is unavailable to and unsought by Macon Dead, senior; what his wife learns to demand from him, and what can never come from the white world as is signified by the inversion of the name of the hospital from Mercy to "no-Mercy." It is only available from within. The center of the narrative is flight; the springboard is mercy.[17]

The first sentence is thus coded with meanings that resonate throughout the novel and indeed point to the circumstances that have shaped the historical experience of African Americans. As Morrison goes on to demonstrate, the kind of reading strategy that she employs in the essay exemplifies the sort of analytic participation she expects from her readers. Such a participatory style of

14

reading breaks down the boundary between reader and text, drawing the reader into the community constructed within the novel
itself. Indeed, such a reading process may be said to be culturally
inflected, for the novel issues a call to which the reader may
choose to respond. Morrison explains:

> The reader as narrator asks the questions the community asks, and
> both reader and "voice" stand among the crowd, within it, with
> privileged intimacy and contact, but without any more privileged
> information than the crowd has. That egalitarianism which places
> us all (reader, the novel's population, the narrator's voice) on the
> same footing reflected for me the force of flight and mercy, and the
> precious, imaginative yet realistic gaze of black people who (at one
> time, anyway) did not mythologize what or whom it myth-
> ologized.[18]

3

Throughout the 1980s, *Song of Solomon* frequently featured promi-
nently in critical studies of African American literature. Its popularity at that time was due, at least in part, to the ways that it
addressed some of the prevailing concerns of that period of African
American literary study: the critique of American individualism
and northern migration, the apparent celebration of folk and oral
culture, and the reclamation of African American history.[19]

One mark of the greatness of the novel has been its ability to
respond to changes in critical concerns and preoccupations as they
have evolved over time. Critics of African American literature have
become increasingly engaged with such topics as constructions of
gender and of black folk practices in narrative and the usefulness of
poststructuralist theories for interpreting black texts.[20] Accordingly, the essays collected here, each written by a leading critic of
Morrison's work, exemplify the fresh theoretical and cultural perspectives that have been brought to bear upon African American
texts in general and upon this work in particular. Each piece in-
cluded here reveals the multifarious complexities contained beneath the surface of a novel that may seem deceptively straightforward given its familiarity. Taken together, the essays in this volume
will spark renewed interest in this pivotal text.

In "From Orality to Literacy: Oral Memory in Toni Morrison's *Song of Solomon*," Joyce Irene Middleton shows how the oral tradition functions in the novel as a mode of resistance against a literacy-based tradition that often renders black life invisible. Her analysis demonstrates how Morrison uses tensions between orality and literacy to undermine pervasive stereotypes and create new possibilities for the representation of African American character. Further, Middleton argues that the novel subtly dismantles metaphors of written memory and moves the reader onto a new terrain where metaphors of orality predominate.

Marilyn Sanders Mobley challenges familiar assumptions about a monolithic black community that recur in interpretations of the novel. In "Call and Response: Voice, Community, and Dialogic Structures in Toni Morrison's *Song of Solomon*," Mobley situates the novel in relation to theoretical discussions developed by Henry Louis Gates Jr., Mikhail Bakhtin, Mae Gwendolyn Henderson, Dale Bauer, and others in order to deepen our understanding of the meanings of voice and community in the text. Her discussion expands as well our understanding of the relation between reader and text that Morrison constructs.

In "Knowing Their Names: Toni Morrison's *Song of Solomon*," Marianne Hirsch discusses ways in which the novel juxtaposes the realities of African American family life to dominant images of the patriarchal family. Drawing on Freudian psychoanalytic theory and a range of discourses about African American families, Hirsch shows that the novel questions the meanings of paternity, patriarchy, and masculinity. Further, her essay examines the construction of racialized gender identities within the community of the novel.

And in "The Postmodernist Rag: Political Identity and the Vernacular in *Song of Solomon*," Wahneema Lubiano shows how the text combines techniques of literary postmodernism with dynamics of African American cultural expression in order to explore the complex positioning of African American individual and collective experience. Within the context of an illuminating meditation upon the place of the vernacular in black postmodernist expression, Lubiano considers the way the novel posits simultaneously the possibility of resistant political identity and a decentered conception of

16

selfhood. Her reading thus problematizes the nature of Milkman's quest and the way that quest has been read by previous critics. In her review of *Jazz,* Deborah E. McDowell has written that "Morrison's entire *oeuvre* has involved a studied effort − to invoke *Ezekiel* − to make the dry and disconnected bones of the black historical past live."[21] Indeed, each of the following essays assumes the significance of African American historical experience to the narrative project of the novel. Moreover, each shows how contemporary literary and cultural theories may expand the interpretive possibilities of the text when it is viewed in relation to the realities and particularities of African American social and cultural practices.

NOTES

1. Nellie McKay, "An Interview with Toni Morrison," *Contemporary Literature* 24 (1983): 426.
2. Toni Morrison, "Unspeakable Things Unspoken: The Afro-American Presence in American Literature," *Michigan Quarterly Review* 28 (1989): 3.
3. Ibid., 9.
4. Ibid., 11.
5. Ibid., 11−12.
6. Toni Morrison, *Playing in the Dark: Whiteness and the Literary Imagination* (Cambridge: Harvard University Press, 1992), 5−6.
7. Toni Morrison, "Rootedness: The Ancestor as Foundation," in *Black Women Writers (1950−1980): A Critical Evaluation,* ed. Mari Evans (New York: Doubleday, Anchor Books, 1984), 341.
8. Gloria Naylor and Toni Morrison, "A Conversation," *Southern Review* 21 (July 1985): 589−90.
9. Susan L. Blake, "Toni Morrison," in *Dictionary of Literary Biography,* vol. 33, *Afro-American Fiction Writers after 1955,* ed. Thadious M. Davis and Trudier Harris (Detroit: Gale Research Co., 1984), 188.
10. Ibid.
11. Naylor and Morrison, "A Conversation," 576.
12. Ibid., 568.
13. Christina Davis, "*Beloved:* A Question of Identity," in *Presence Africaine* 145 (1988): 144.
14. My summary of Morrison's analysis does not do full justice to the

complexity of her reading. Readers should examine her discussion in detail for themselves.

15. Morrison, "Unspeakable Things," 27, 28–9.
16. Ibid., 28.
17. Ibid., 27.
18. Ibid., 29.
19. See, for instance, Bonnie J. Barthold, *Black Time: Fiction of Africa, the Caribbean, and the United States* (New Haven: Yale University Press, 1981); Jane Campbell, *Mythic Black Fiction: The Transformation of History* (Knoxville: University of Tennessee Press, 1986); Melvin Dixon, *Ride Out the Wilderness: Geography and Identity in Afro-American Literature* (Urbana and Chicago: University of Illinois Press, 1987); Genevieve Fabre, "Genealogical Archaeology or the Quest for Legacy in Toni Morrison's *Song of Solomon,*" in *Critical Essays on Toni Morrison,* ed. Nellie Y. McKay (Boston: G. K. Hall, 1988), 105–14; Valerie Smith, "The Quest for and Discovery of Identity in Toni Morrison's *Song of Solomon,*" *Southern Review* 21 (1985): 721–32.
20. See, for instance, Kimberly W. Benston, "Re-weaving the 'Ulysses Scene': Enchantment, Post-Oedipal Identity, and the Buried Text of Blackness in Toni Morrison's *Song of Solomon,*" in *Comparative American Identities: Race, Sex, and Nationality in the Modern Text,* ed. Hortense J. Spillers (New York: Routledge, 1991), 87–109.
21. Deborah E. McDowell, "Harlem Nocturne," *Women's Review of Books* 9 (June 1992): 3.

2

From Orality to Literacy: Oral Memory in Toni Morrison's *Song of Solomon*

JOYCE IRENE MIDDLETON

IN a frequently cited passage in Plato's *Phaedrus*, Socrates tells his young student an Egyptian tale to support his strong argument against writing. In the dialogue a king argues with the Egyptian god who invented writing, declaiming its detrimental effects on the human memory and the art of memory:

> The fact is that this invention will produce forgetfulness in the souls of those who have learned it. They will not need to exercise their memories, being able to rely on what is written, calling things to mind no longer from within themselves by their own unaided powers, but under the stimulus of external marks that are alien to themselves. So it's not a recipe for memory, but for reminding, that you have discovered. And as for wisdom, you're equipping your pupils with only a semblance of it, not with truth. Thanks to you and your invention, your pupils will be widely read without benefit of a teacher's instruction; in consequence, they'll entertain the delusion that they have wide knowledge, while they are, in fact, for the most part incapable of real judgment. They will also be difficult to get on with since they will have become wise merely in their own conceit, not genuinely so. (1956, 68–9)

In addition to these Socratic arguments, many fourth and fifth century records mirror the stage when Greeks heatedly debated the use and influence of writing and alphabetic literacy in their culture. How the story ends is old news: writing wins a dominant role in the Western history of discourse, and speechmaking gradually loses its prominence in language pedagogy. But the story of literacy, despite this evolutionary victory, offers no resolution to these early concerns about the loss of the art of memory. Thus, these dormant and lingering oral language issues, now over 2,000 years old, have reasserted their significance to language and literary studies.

19

Eric Havelock points out in his *Preface to Plato* that the spread of literacy did not replace the Greek oral consciousness all at once. The art of memory, in particular, was part of the tradition of Western letters and rhetoric well into the seventeenth century, as Frances Yates's well-known work *The Art of Memory* documents. Speech continues to be a language of privilege in relation to writing. Furthermore, the care and cultivation of the human memory, through formal rhetorical training, mnemonics, and practice, are an index to the degree of a culture's "residual orality," the implicit value for the spoken word in a culture that writes (Ong 1982, 109).

The existence within a culture of an enormous range of systems used to train the human memory reveals that culture's expansive sense of language and its powers. Mental picturing in memory, spatial or architectural memory, memory from sight, memory from sound, the effect of emotions on the memory, and the arrangement of impressions, of kinds of metaphors, and of principles of association – these and other mnemonic techniques contributed to classical rhetorical theories and the teaching of memory and recollection (Yates 1966, 27–69). Bruno Gentili describes the uses and effects of memory in the classical poetic tradition in his *Poetry and Its Public in Ancient Greece* (1988). During performances, Gentili notes, the memories of both poet and audience are involved in "sympathetic 'magic'" (1988, 51). Features of this oral poetic tradition – reminding us of Walter Ong's reference to the "high somatic component" of oral memory (1982, 67–8) – include the "talking picture," the "speaking dance," and the representation of "emotional states through rhythmical [auditory] and visual effects" (Gentili 1988, 52–3). For composition, or what Gentili calls "poetics as heuristic imitation" (1988, 54), poets draw on these oral features "from a mnemonic repertory to provide [either] the subject matter of myth or, at a linguistic level, lexemes and stylemes" (1988, 53). Oral memory, in contrast to textual memory, depends completely upon formulas, rituals, and other oral art forms to strengthen recalling and retelling stories. Both singer and interpreter of song, the bard draws on oral memory to perform and appeals to the oral memory of the hearer in order to aid the hearer's remembrance. But whether linked to the tradition of classical rhetoric or to that of the inspired poet, the central role of memory, as Havelock tells us, was to preserve cultural knowledge (1963, 100). These descriptions of ancient mnemonic arts help to create an interdisciplinary vocabulary for analyzing orality, literacy, and the art of memory.

The exceptional continuity of the art of memory in the literary production of black writers moves us to recall the African American's orientation to reading and writing in this country. Slaves knew that they had to steal their literacy – since it was illegal to learn to read – and many did. In a fairly recent account of slaves who learned to read, Janet Cornelius tells us, "Despite the dangers and difficulties, thousands of slaves learned to read and write in the antebellum South" (1983, 171). Verbal testimonies and other documentation illustrate the secrecy and deception that formed the slaves' social context for achieving literacy. Learning to read demands an intensive use of memory. In one example, Cornelius discusses a slave named Belle Caruthers, whose duties were "to fan her mistress and to nurse the baby." She continued, "the baby had alphabet blocks to play with and I learned my letters while she learned hers" (1983, 180). Cornelius cites another slave woman's deceptive method for learning to read:

> Moses Slaughter's mother, the housekeeper, would say to the owner's daughter, "Come here, Emily, Mamma will keep your place for you," and while little Emily read, "Mamma Emalina" followed each line until she too was a fluent reader and could teach her own children. (1983, 180)

Frederick Douglass's *Narrative* gives another description of using deceptive strategies to attain literacy skills. He tells us that

> when I met with any boy who I knew could write, I would tell him that I could write as well as he. The next word would be, "I don't believe you. Let me see you try it." I would then write the letters which I had been so fortunate as to learn, and ask him to beat that. In this way I got a good many lessons in writing, which it is quite possible I should never have gotten in any other way. (1987, 281)

Of course, Douglass's primary desire was for freedom, power, and a better quality of life, and literacy was then and continues to be an essential means to those ends. These African American experiences in relation to literacy help illustrate the inherent tensions between orality and literacy and the cultural conflicts in Toni Morrison's *Song of Solomon.*

Reviewing the historical continuum on the uses of Western literacy, we see the story of Plato's *Phaedrus* unfold: as literacy advances, the art of memory wanes. But in contrast, we also see that the tenacity of the oral tradition in African American culture reveals, *as any oral culture would,* characteristic features of the art of memory in its literary tradition. One might think immediately of the storehouse of folklore, cultural commonplaces, and oral language devices that create the fabric of a cultural or communal memory. But given the extensive body of documented research and literature on that subject,[1] I concentrate instead on the enabling power that African American writers give their readers, such as a power for recalling and inventing their own stories. The art of memory that I am analyzing in Toni Morrison's work focuses on significant compositional techniques: the weaving of the oral and written texts and the subtle shapes, forms, rhythms, and rhetorical topics that evoke compelling psychic reflections and responses. Since the art of an oral tradition in the novel invests itself in the reader as a participant, I will articulate descriptions of memory, writing, and reader involvement.

A brief introductory example will illustrate oral poetic features in a literary text and illuminate Morrison's literary efforts. Chapter 11 of *Song of Solomon* ends at an important moment of growth in the life of Milkman Dead, the central character. But instead of delivering a lengthy narration, the storyteller presents this significant episode in only three brief paragraphs. Away from his home, Milkman is offered a place to rest and is invited to take a bath at the home of a young woman named Sweet, whose name is indeed allegorical. The bath, in the tradition of oral and bardic storytelling, is a ritual, and accordingly, the storyteller uses ritual language – "a fixed pattern of utterances" (Carter 1991, 212) – to frame the occasion of this ritual that celebrates the beauty of life and loving. In this story the bathing ritual communicates rebirth: Milkman discovers giving and sharing, new meaning in a loving relationship

22

with a woman. Milkman offers to give Sweet a cool bath, and the passage flows seductively:

> He soaped and rubbed her until her skin squeaked and glistened like onyx. She put salve on his face. He washed her hair. She sprinkled talcum on his feet. He straddled her behind and massaged her back. She put witch hazel on his swollen neck. He made up the bed. She gave him gumbo to eat. He washed the dishes. She washed his clothes and hung them out to dry. He scoured her tub. She ironed his shirt and pants. He gave her fifty dollars. She kissed his mouth. He touched her face. She said please come back. He said I'll see you tonight. (288–9)

This bath scene signifies Milkman's cultural immersion in a black, traditional oral culture. The ritual frame creates a pause in the time of the narrative flow in the novel. The verbal economy and rhythm in this passage are immediately noticeable, but the skillful presentation by this storyteller subtly, yet powerfully, persuades the audience to remember the meaning of this ritual frame. The rhythm that we feel in the physical motions of these two characters harmonizes with the rhythm of the storyteller's language. In traditional oral epic poetry, Havelock would describe this aspect of the storyteller's appeal to the audience's oral memory as rhythmic hypnosis (1978, 38), poetry performed in such a way (and usually enhanced with music) that the episode survives in the memories of the hearers. Most memorable in Morrison's significant passage is its movement and its intimacy: a dialogic, shifting focus (he/she), bodily gestures, complementary movements (forward/backward), and lots of touching.

The audience finds pleasure in this brief passage because the storyteller, as Morrison tells us, has left spaces, planned spaces, that can be filled in, and "into these spaces should fall the ruminations of the reader and his or her invented or recollected or misunderstood knowingness" (1989, 29). The seductive weaving of this text – with its familiar human content (everyone takes a bath) and human emotions – engages the oral memory of the readers to interpret the silences and celebrate the significant action in this episode. Thus, the reader is implicated in the tale, just as the bard's audience participated in his interactive performance. In an earlier essay, "Memory, Creation, and Writing," Morrison commented on this special kind of relationship that she wants to achieve with her readers:

> I want my fiction to urge the reader into active participation in the non-narrative, nonliterary experience of the text. . . .
> I want [the reader] to respond on the same plane as an illiterate or preliterate [person] would. I want to subvert [the reader's] traditional comfort so that [he or she] may experience an unorthodox one: that of being in the company of [his or her] own imagination. (1984, 387)

Milkman wears a new psychic garment at the end of this passage, and the verbal economy, the repetition, the sensual concrete imagery, the additive feature of the text (as Ong would describe it), and the simple shape of this game-playing language give us an intimate utterance and generate an image of change in Milkman's behavior and character that will be important to later action in the tale.

In *From Folklore to Fiction* (1988), H. Nigel Thomas explores the uses of rituals in African American fiction and analyzes the role of ritual in the novel. One fairly common literary theme is that materialism taints rituals, and rituals are linked to group survival (1988, 174). Thomas places *Song of Solomon* in the *cante fable* tradition of the African American folktale performance: "The meaning of the story [the traditional oral folktale] is the principal point of the novel, coming only when ancestral wisdom is relearned and ancestral obligations fulfilled" (1988, 177). Thus Morrison's novel as ritual transforms an old folktale and attempts "to clear a pathway from the dense jungle of materialism back to the source of ancestral wisdom" (1988, 177). In *Song of Solomon*, memory and intimacy are prerequisites for gaining ancestral knowledge and personal wisdom. Morrison's readers observe how literacy, a means to success and power in the external, material, and racist world, alienates Macon Dead's family from their older cultural and family rituals, their inner spiritual lives, and their oral memories.

Zora Neale Hurston's work on the character of African American language helps to further illustrate these kinds of tensions between oral and literate cultures. In "Characteristics of Negro Expression," Hurston compares the values of oral and literate traditions of language and asserts that "the white man thinks in written language and the Negro thinks in hieroglyphics" (1981a, 50), that is, thinks semiotically with respect to the English language and writing. By articulating two different perceptions of language, one that is strictly alphabetic and one that is imagistic, Hurston's descriptions help us uncover conflicts and analyze the agonistically toned, dualistic tensions that are felt in Morrison's black community.

In "The Sanctified Church," another anthropological essay on black culture and language by Hurston, the author links conceptions of orality to the qualities of music or song.

> In the mouth of the Negro the English language loses its stiffness, yet conveys its meaning accurately. . . . "The **booming bounderries** [*sic*] of this **wh**irling **w**orld" conveys just as accurate a picture as mere "boundaries," and a little music is gained besides. (1981b, 81; emphasis added)

Music, of course, strengthens the auditory, associative, oral memory. We might recall the importance of music, rhythm, and lyricism in *Song of Solomon* when the main character, Milkman, memorizes the song that unlocks the key to his family history. But more significantly, music – songs and numerous similes – resonates throughout *Song of Solomon*, sustaining an exquisite intermingling of prose and poetry.

There are several key moments in the novel when Morrison's storyteller focuses on oral–literate tensions. Three of Morrison's characters – Macon Dead, First Corinthians, and Milkman – show how their social and political conceptions of oral and written language either empower them or render them spiritually, socially, or emotionally impotent. Because of their conceptions, these characters either cultivate or suppress the communal and inner voices that privilege their personal, auditory, and associative memory.

For example, when Macon Dead Sr., the grandson of the mythic flying African, recalls and interprets his father's fate, telling his story to Milkman, he clearly views his father as a victim of illiteracy, but significantly, he also associates literacy with property, ownership, and material success:

> Papa couldn't read, couldn't even sign his name. Had a mark he used. They tricked him. He signed something, I don't know what, and they told him they owned his property. He never read nothing. I tried to teach him, but he said he couldn't remember those little

marks from one day to the next. Wrote one word in his life – Pilate's name; copied it out of the Bible. That's what she got folded up in that earring. He should have let me teach him. Everything bad that ever happened to him happened because he couldn't read. (53)

Through Macon's focus on his father's illiteracy, we can understand his passion for the letter. His desire for empowerment is a clear choice at an unknown cost, and we must remember that he was still a young man when he saw white men murder his father with a shotgun. But Macon Dead's assumptions about literacy and power – that his father was a loser because of his illiteracy, that the "little marks" should bear some mnemonic power, despite the father's complaints, and that the son, who misunderstands his own oral–literate tensions, should teach the father – reveal an implicit cultural irony about orality, literacy, and empowerment if we compare Macon's image of his father as powerless to the man who is portrayed by the narrator at the beginning of the novel naming Pilate.

The illiterate father, Jake, the son of Solomon (who later becomes the first Macon Dead because of errors on a written record), picks a word from the Bible, a "group of letters that seemed to him strong and handsome; saw in them a large figure that looked like a tree hanging in some princely but protective way over a row of smaller trees" (18). Here we see that the father "thinks in hieroglyphics," as Hurston describes this. Arguing with the midwife and drawing on the power of his own emotional reasoning, the father insists that "Pilate," "the name of the man that killed Jesus" (19), will be the name of his motherless child. It is not due to his illiteracy or ignorance that the father insists upon Pilate's name. The midwife, obviously a reader, voices the authority of the text not only by explaining what the selected word means but also by attempting to persuade the father that he has made a wrong choice. But the father resists that authority: he does not automatically submit to the authorized version of the biblical text. Rather, he dares to question the significance of that textual authority for his present purposes.

As we trace the meaning of this event throughout the novel, the naming ritual reveals its transcendent quality: the father's writing of Pilate's name symbolizes the energy and familial bonding between the father and his daughter and, in the scene of her death, the eternal, spiritual life of the woman named Pilate, when the bird flies away with her earring. Without the cultural tensions that his son experiences, the father draws images freely from the well of his own personal, oral memory and imagination. The crime and loss of the father's property due to his illiteracy and to racism are undeniable. But the personal dignity and clarity that the father reveals are also a valuable part of the family legacy that Milkman eventually discovers.

Thinking hieroglyphically, the father reveals a unique creativity that merges oral and written traditions in this cultural naming ritual. In addition, the father's responses at the naming of Pilate reveal the same kind of cultural energy, an agonistic expression of signifying as Gates (1988) and others describe it, that the community asserts in the political conflict over naming "Doctor Street" and "Not Doctor Street" or "Mercy Hospital" and "No Mercy Hospital" at the beginning of this novel. Through these agonistic responses to racial exploitation, the black community outwits and resists the attempts of the white literate authority to usurp the indigenous authority of the people who actually live in the community and their oral tradition. Thus, Morrison effectively problematizes oral–literate tensions so that her readers will explore new meanings in the significance of oral and literate cultural experiences.

Following an ambition that always points toward material wealth and success, Macon Dead, the grandson of the mythic flying African, finds considerable satisfaction, and he learns to ignore and suppress the inner, cultural voices of survival from his past. But occasionally, his oral memory stirs his desire for song, warmth, intimacy, and rituals. Feeling tired and irritable one evening, feeling like "an outsider" and like a "landless wanderer" (27), Macon finds himself turning away from his own house, thinking sorrowfully, "There was *no music* there" (29; emphasis added). Instead of going to his house, he walks toward the home of Pilate, his only sister, who sings eloquent blues in a powerful contralto, for "tonight he wanted just a bit of music – from the person who had been his first caring for" (29). In this scene, Morrison's storyteller focuses on the lack of music in Macon's home life. At first only listening, and then later peering through a window in the dark, Macon, eavesdropping, muses upon the ceremonial scene in Pilate's home:

> They were singing some melody that Pilate was leading. A phrase that the other two were taking up and building on. Her powerful contralto, Reba's piercing soprano in counterpoint, and the soft voice of the girl, Hagar, . . . pulled him like a carpet tack under the influence of a magnet.
> *Surrendering to the sound,* Macon moved closer. He wanted no conversation, no witness, only to listen and perhaps to see the three of them, the source of that music that made him think of fields and wild turkey and calico. . . . Near the window, hidden by the dark, he felt the irritability of the day drain from him and relished the effortless beauty of the women singing in the candlelight. . . . As Macon felt himself softening under the weight of *memory and music,* the song died down. The air was quiet and yet Macon Dead could not leave. He liked looking at them freely this way. (30; emphasis added)

Outside Pilate's home, Macon witnesses the songs and rituals of a ceremony. He is a distant observer. But seduced by the music and stimulated by his oral memory, he actively participates in the ceremony, as his quiet peaceful feelings reveal. Brief reflections such as these show us the cultural tensions and distance between Macon's boyhood rituals and freedom – the emotional wealth of his youth – and the materialistic values to which he adheres as a man. Through these stories of Macon Dead and his father, Morrison's storyteller moves her readers to question Western assumptions about discredited sources of knowledge and familiar images of power. Who is actually empowered in these stories, Macon Dead, whose keys and property symbolize his literacy, or his illiterate father, the son of a cultural hero, the flying American named Solomon, also spelled Shalimar?

I note the variant spelling and pronunciation of Solomon/Shalimar here because it illustrates another cultural conflict between an oral and literate community. Walter Ong encourages those of us immersed in literate conventions to reconsider the conventions of spelling – exactness – whose establishment was a primary activity in the eighteenth century. If we place the two names, Solomon and Shalimar, side by side, our visual readings

would first note the differences in spelling. But Morrison constructs the oral–aural experience in this novel so that similarities in
sounds provide crucial, coherent links in Milkman's search for his
family's wealth. As we follow Milkman in his travels, as he gets
closer and closer to the site in Virginia that holds local knowledge
for him, learning through listening is a seminal part of his experience. In the "heart and soul of Shalimar, Virginia" (263), a small
town uncharted on a map, Milkman discovers that "[e]ven the
name of the town sounded like Solomon: Shalimar, which Mr.
Solomon and everybody else pronounced **Shalleemone**" (305).
In this sentence, Morrison presents three variant spellings for
which the alphabetic or phonetic rendering is obviously irrelevant.
Morrison's wordplay throws into relief the significance of sound
and listening in black cultural expression.

In fact, Morrison disarms her readers' sense of oral and written
differences with a considerable number of puns and wordplay in
riddles and humorous passages throughout this novel. In several
instances, she uses wordplay directly related to the underlying
flying-African myth of her tale. Milkman, swimming in a natural
pool and elated about his discovery that his ancestor was a flying
African, exclaims: "That motherfucker could fly! Could fly! He
didn't need no airplane. Didn't need no fucking tee double you ay.
He could fly his own self!" (328). Here Morrison converts the
familiar visual acronym into an acoustic, phonetic spelling – an
imitation of an utterance and a subtle means of promoting the
"aural" quality of her storytelling. The use of homonyms throughout the novel, such as the wordplay on Pilate's name ("like an
airplane pilot?"), also emphasizes the oral/aural quality of Morrison's writing. In effect, Morrison privileges orality so that her
readers can hear and feel the unique oral character of African
American language use and see how the survival of cultural consciousness, or nomos,[2] is preserved in a highly literate culture.
From both an oral and a literate perspective, then, the motif of
naming has an explicit and a very powerful implicit meaning in
this novel.

The story of First Corinthians Dead in Chapter 9 illustrates the
effects of traditional Western literate values on her consciousness
and oral memory. Both black and a woman, she suffers a dual

powerlessness. Her father, black but a man, is successful in ways that she cannot be, despite her highly literate training. With potent irony, Morrison describes First Corinthians's predicament:

> Bryn Mawr had done what a four-year dose of liberal education was designed to do: unfit her for eighty percent of the useful work of the world. First, by training her for leisure time, enrichments, and domestic mindlessness. Second, by a clear implication that she was too good for such work. After graduation she returned to a work world in which colored girls, regardless of their background, were in demand for one and only one kind of work. (190)

First Corinthians was employed as a maid for the city's poet laureate, Michael-Mary Graham, but she tells her mother that she is employed as an amanuensis, which sounds important. Historical context illuminates the irony of the passive, receptive role of the amanuensis, who, as a mere transcriber, was always held in low regard by teachers of classical rhetoric and who, later in the history of Western letters, was a person of low social and political status, similar to the historical status of women. We might recall the status of Milton's daughters in this regard.

Racial and class barriers are also significant social influences for First Corinthians Dead, and she explicitly confronts issues of class and her image of social superiority throughout this episode. But there is also a considerable focus in this chapter on how much her background in schooling and her highly literate training contribute to her belief in her superior self-image. First Corinthians is fluent in, not one, but two Western literate traditions, English and French. She did not attend a historically black college or university, such as "Fisk, Howard, Talledega, [or] Tougaloo" (189) for her training, but instead she attended Bryn Mawr, a racially integrated institution where she would clearly have been a "minority" student immersed in the study of Western literacy. This background elevates First Corinthians. Her education teaches her "to contribute to the civilization — or in her case, the civilizing — of her community" (188). In addition, there are numerous references to bring into focus the world of the book, to briefly sketch the life, tastes, and cultural habits of the city's poet laureate and to portray cultural conflicts that are linked to literacy.

The forceful argument with Henry Porter in which First Corinthians attempts to distinguish herself from "those women on the bus . . . the only people she knew for certain she was superior to" (197) provides a close illustration of the oral–literate, agonistic gesturing in this chapter. Emotionally, she argues that those women would

> love to have a greeting card dropped in their lap. . . . But oh, I forgot. You couldn't do that, could you, because they wouldn't be able to read it. They'd have to take it home and wait till Sunday and give it to the preacher to read it to them. Of course when they heard it they might not know what it meant. But it wouldn't matter — they'd see the flowers and the curlicues all over the words and they'd be happy. It wouldn't matter a bit that it was the most ridiculous, most clichéd, most commercial piece of tripe the drugstore world has to offer. They wouldn't know mediocrity if it punched them right in their fat faces. (197)

Noticeably, Morrison does not privilege the voice of the oral consciousness in this argument. We do not hear from or know anything about "those women." Thus the hierarchical, literate consciousness that First Corinthians represents in her criticisms seems to prevail in the structure of this argument. But First Corinthians does not say anything significantly concrete or "close to the human lifeworld" (Ong 1982, 42) about the women to whom she feels superior. She fictionalizes them ("they'd see the flowers and . . . they'd be happy") and uses clichés and stereotyped images ("they'd give [the card] to the preacher to read it") in order to invent the arguments that support her views of superiority. It is from this hierarchical and distanced position that she too easily critiques their inabilities. The argument about literacy and class proves to be ineffectual. But at this moment in the story, it brings into focus the kind of fictionalizing about her own life that First Corinthians later begins to confront.

The significance of these social tensions is that First Corinthians, the great-granddaughter of the flying African, cannot tell anyone her stories. She has no audience. Despite her broad and valuable cultural exposure and refinement, Western literate values place a mask of abstraction on her life in the black community. Viewed semiotically, her role as an amanuensis reveals a mask that con-

31

strains her self-expressions and blocks her social channels. She cannot tell her mother the truth about her job. She dare not reveal to her boss that she speaks fluent French. She must hide her love affair with a yardman who works for her father. With these constraints, we see that race, class, and her social conceptions of literacy negate her ability to cultivate what Toni Cade Bambara calls a "personal mythology" (1989). Like her father, who learns to suppress his oral memory, she too learns to suppress and ignore the real value and meaning in the stories of her life. Instead of recognizing and fulfilling her own desires and motivations, she becomes a forty-four-year-old baby doll. But unlike her father, First Corinthians becomes aware of her mask. In a pivotal moment of her life, she walks toward her home but then, self-consciously, runs away from it, just as her father did in an earlier scene. Emotions and memory move her thoughts and body from a wild frenzy to catharsis, as her oral memory of the past sheds light on her present tensions:

> Corinthians ran toward [her lover's car] faster than she had ever run in her life, faster than she'd cut across the grass on Honoré Island when she was five and the whole family went there for a holiday. Faster even than the time she flew down the stairs having seen for the first time what the disease had done to her grandfather. (198)

Finding the car locked, rapping and pounding failing to awaken her sleeping lover, First Corinthians

> climbed up on the fender and lay full out across the hood of the car. She didn't look through the windshield at him. She just lay there, stretched across the car, her fingers struggling for a grip on steel. She thought of nothing. Nothing except what her body needed to do to hang on, to never let go. Even if he drove off at one hundred miles an hour, she would hang on. (200)

In this dramatic context, we see that her lover, Henry Porter, is her antagonist, enabling her to confront her cultural tensions and saving her from the imminent "smothering death" (200) that surrounds her life. She must stop denying her own emotional reality. She must stop living her material life as a literate "other." Through her antagonist, First Corinthians faces herself as a woman with "fake feelings" (196) who uses a distanced "reading voice" (196) even when she speaks to those who care deeply for her and who feels superior to others because of her social conceptions of literacy. First Corinthians develops confidence and skill in her "intellectual intelligence," but she suppresses her "emotional intelligence," as Morrison would describe this distinction (Davis 1988, 142). In this pivotal, dramatic scene – with an explosion of primal emotions – the feelings stored in the well of her oral memory pour forth relentlessly, rupturing and crumbling her mask of abstraction. She begins to assume ownership of her own language. What she achieves, and what her father could not, is the ability to recognize, *name*, and act on her cultural contradictions.

Song of Solomon tells, among many other tales, a story of family distance and loss of cultural knowledge through generational migration. Staging a series of rituals and illustrating powerful images of oral memory in the black community, the novel focuses on the significance of these losses. The story of Milkman represents the act of reconstituting the memory of the past with the experiences of the present. But he must learn how to listen. As Joseph Skerrett describes him, Milkman "lacks a connecting imagination" (1985, 194). During his search for his family's inheritance, Milkman finds Circe, "the oldest Black woman in the world," as Morrison fondly describes her (1984, 387). But Circe tells Milkman, with love and criticism in her voice: "You don't listen to people. Your ear is on your head, but it's not connected to your brain" (247). With her own ancestral wisdom, Circe helps Morrison's readers understand that in "the process of storytelling, speaking and listening refer to realities that do not involve just the imagination. The speech is seen, heard, smelled, tasted, and touched. It destroys, brings into life, nurtures" (Trinh 1987, 5). This deeper understanding of the African American oral tradition illuminates the potential problems that oral and literate cultural tensions create with regard to uses of language and the human memory.

Milkman listens to many, many stories, and the African cultural arts of listening and remembering are central to Milkman's success in the scene when he unlocks the secret to his family's riddle that found permanence and perpetual transmission in a children's game song:

The children were starting the round again. . . .
Milkman's scalp began to tingle. . . .
He sat up and waited for the children to begin the verse again. "Come booba yalle, come booba tambee," it sounded like, and didn't make sense. But another line – "Black lady fell down on the ground" – was clear enough. There was another string of nonsense words, then "Threw her body all around." . . .
. . . The verse ended in another clear line. "Twenty-one children, the last one *Jake!*" [Morrison's emphasis] . . . Now Milkman understood. . . .
Milkman took out his wallet and pulled from it his airplane ticket stub, *but he had no pencil to write with, and his pen was in his suit. He would just have to listen and memorize it.* He closed his eyes and concentrated while the children, inexhaustible in their willingness to repeat a *rhythmic, rhyming action game, performed the round over and over again.* And Milkman memorized all of what they sang. (305–6; emphasis added)

At this important moment in the story, Milkman cannot simply write the song down, as his literate impulses move him to do. If he wants the knowledge, he must commit the song to his personal, oral memory, just as his slave and African ancestors had done, not to an artificial, external memory – a written record. As Trinh Minh-Ha notes in her studies on African culture: "To listen carefully is to preserve" (1987, 4).

Toni Morrison's strongest illustration of cultural oral memory in *Song of Solomon* takes place in the scene of the hunt when Milkman observes the finely tuned listening and communicating skills of his partner, Calvin, and the other men on the hunt. The pitch dark setting renders his body invisible, even to himself. In this environment, sound reigns over sight. Sitting underneath a sweet gum tree, Milkman discovers what his ancestors understood about language, before alphabetic, literate language. While listening to all the varying sounds in the woods, Milkman begins to remember his "ancient properties" (the phrase Morrison uses for ancestral knowledge and black cultural tradition in *Tar Baby*):

All those shrieks, those rapid tumbling barks, the long sustained yells, the tuba sounds, the drumbeat sounds, the low liquid **howm howm,** the reedy whistles, the thin **eeeee's** of a cornet, the **unh unh unh** bass chords. It was all language. . . . No, it was not language; it was what there was before language. Before things were written down. (281)

The emphasis on tonal semantics and on the musical sensibility about language reminds us, once again, of Hurston's observations on the aural quality of African American language as a significant component of oral memory in black culture. In this passage, Morrison also moves her readers to consider the deep effects of what Ong calls the interiority of sound: "I am at the center of my auditory world, which envelopes me, establishing me at a kind of core of sensation and existence" (1982, 71–2). Milkman's immersion in this auditory experience awakens his dormant listening skills to new language experiences and ways of knowing. Milkman's experiences – of the woods, hunters, killing – move him to use his preliterate imagination to reclaim his unlettered ancestors' skill for listening: an intuitive and sensual ability to converse with animals and with nature. The scene of the hunt represents a ritual reenactment of this ancient cultural knowledge. In fact, this new knowledge saves his life:

> Feeling both tense and relaxed, he sank his fingers into the grass. He tried to listen with his fingertips, to hear what, if anything, the earth had to say, and it told him quickly that someone was standing behind him and he had just enough time to raise one hand to his neck and catch the wire that fastened around his throat. (282)

Milkman's process of relearning the personal value of his own orality culminates in the final, celebratory scene in this novel. After Pilate's death, Milkman offers words of praise in a scene that draws on the feelings of an oral epic. Milkman rises from his knees, following what Skerrett describes as his "recitation to the griot" (1985, 201), a moment which holds powerful implications for viewing Pilate as a culture bearer. Trinh Minh-Ha notes, "Every *griotte* who dies, as it is said in Africa, is a whole library that burns down (a 'library in which the archives are not classified but are completely inventoried')" (1987, 5). Milkman's monument to Pilate is in the form of a song rather than in stone, contrasting oral and written forms of cultural inscription and memory.[3] Having fulfilled the death ritual, Milkman rises and calls out in the dark for Guitar, his beloved friend driven mad by material greed for gold and by internalized racism.[4] From the grand height and spectacle of Solomon's Leap, overlooking a dark, lush natural setting, Milkman engages in a symbolic instance of the African American cultural call and response (Smitherman 1977, 104–18) with Nature herself participating and listening to this tale:

> "Guitar!" he shouted.
> *Tar tar tar,* said the hills.
> "Over here, brother man! Can you see me?" Milkman cupped his mouth with one hand and waved the other over his head. "Here I am!"
> *Am am am am,* said the rocks.
> "You want me? Huh? You want my life?"
> *Life life life life.*
> . . . [Guitar appears.] As fleet and bright as a lodestar he wheeled toward Guitar and it did not matter which one of them would give up the ghost in the killing arms of his brother. For now he knew what Shalimar [Solomon] knew: If you surrendered to the air, you could *ride* it. (341)

The acoustic effect of this passage structures the call and response pattern. This oral language style underscores the harmony that Milkman has achieved: he is no longer separate from, no longer isolated from, the life-sustaining knowledge of his past. His allegorical flight is inward for we have seen him find self-knowledge, especially the oral nature of his ancient roots, and we have seen him acquire a deep value for life and for human relationships.

A lingering irony found in Plato's arguments against writing is that his criticisms are preserved only because he wrote them. Toni Morrison creates her work in the center of that irony. Merging Greek, biblical, and African American oral traditions in *Song of Solomon,* Morrison brings orality and literacy face to face and throws significant cultural conflicts into relief. *Song of Solomon* illustrates the oral tradition as a conveyor of cultural values, ideas, heroes, and accomplishments that are often in direct conflict with schooling and literate training, where the written word renders African American history invisible. The storyteller uses the tensions between orality and literacy, the chords and discords in the language, to deconstruct the stereotypes and myths that permeate the black American experience, and in the new spaces she sketches new myths. She also deconstructs the hierarchical language meta-phor that privileges the linear consciousness of literacy by moving her readers beyond the framework of written memory into the reaches of the intimate, nonlinear, somatic oral memory. The sus-tained lyricism in this lengthy novel – its songs, metaphors, and similes – seduces the readers' oral memory to recall and retell the tale. And like a good jazz performance, Morrison's *Song of Solomon* tells a story "for which the appropriate mode of the interpreter is to make *remembrance* . . . predominate over memorization . . . and for which each performance instigates a new integrity" (Zumthor 1990, 181). Her bardic voice, with its skillful control of episodic delivery and flashbacks, reveals the universal and unique energy of the black community. Through her playful intermingling of an ancient, oral storytelling genre with a modern literate one, Toni Morrison draws on the creative dimensions of both oral and liter-ate language, giving us new and stimulating perspectives on oral memory in her accomplished modern novel.

NOTES

1. Trudier Harris's *Fiction and Folklore* (1991), for example, provides a focused study of folklore in Morrison's novels. Gayl Jones's *Liberating Voices* (1991) analyzes the technical effects of the oral tradition in Afri-can American literature, and H. Nigel Thomas in *From Folklore to Fiction* (1988) analyzes the varied ways in which African American authors use and transform the oral tradition in their fiction.
2. Discussing the uses of the oral epic in his *The Greek Concept of Justice,* Eric Havelock defines "nomos" as "the custom-laws, the folkways, the habits of a people" (1978, 24). He also writes that a "preliterate culture uses epic not only for entertainment but as a storage mechanism which conserves the ethos and nomos of the culture . . . . the oral style puts a heavy premium upon those verbal devices which encourage memoriz-ation" (1978, 220).
3. The analogy between monuments of stone and monuments of song in Greek poetry is discussed in Segal 1989, 330–59.
4. We should note that Guitar, like Macon Dead Sr., also helps to illustrate the agonistic responses to the problems created by oral–literate cultur-al tensions in this novel. As a child he challenges a white, adult wom-an, a nurse, to correct her spelling of the word "admissions" because

37

she forgot an *s* in her instructions when she directed him to find the security guard at the back of the hospital. The focus of Guitar's response is on the literate rule, but as his grandmother, who could easily be illiterate, points out to him, the nurse also forgot to say "please" (7).

WORKS CITED

Bambara, Toni Cade. 1989. "On Keeping a Dream Notebook." Creative Writing Workshop, Pennsylvania State University.

Carter, Michael F. 1991. "The Ritual Functions of Epideictic Rhetoric: The Case of Socrates' Funeral Oration." *Rhetorica* 9:209–32.

Cornelius, Janet. 1983. "'We Slipped and Learned to Read': Slave Accounts of the Literacy Process, 1830–1865." *Phylon* 44:171–85.

Davis, Christina. 1988. "Interview with Toni Morrison." *Presence Africaine* 145 (July): 141–50.

Douglass, Frederick. 1987. *Narrative of the Life of Frederick Douglass.* In *The Classic Slave Narratives,* ed. Henry Louis Gates Jr. New York: Signet.

Gates, Henry Louis, Jr. 1988. *The Signifying Monkey.* New York: Oxford University Press.

Gentili, Bruno. 1988. *Poetry and Its Public in Ancient Greece: From Homer to the Fifth Century.* Trans. A. Thomas Cole. Baltimore: Johns Hopkins University Press.

Harris, Trudier. 1991. *Fiction and Folklore.* Knoxville: University of Tennessee Press.

Havelock, Eric. 1978. *The Greek Concept of Justice.* Cambridge: Harvard University Press.

———. 1963. *Preface to Plato.* Cambridge: Harvard University Press.

Hurston, Zora Neale. 1981a. "Characteristics of Negro Expression." In *The Sanctified Church,* 49–68. Berkeley: Turtle Island Press.

———. 1981b. "The Sanctified Church." In *The Sanctified Church,* 79–107. Berkeley: Turtle Island Press.

Jones, Gayl. 1991. *Liberating Voices: Oral Tradition in African American Literature.* Cambridge: Harvard University Press.

Minh-Ha, Trinh T. 1987. "Grandma's Story." In *Blasted Allegories,* ed. Brian Wallis, 2–31. Cambridge: MIT Press.

Morrison, Toni. 1984. "Memory, Creation, and Writing." *Thought* 59 (December): 385–90.

———. "Unspeakable Things Unspoken: The Afro-American Presence in American Literature." *Michigan Quarterly Review* 28 (Winter): 1–34.

Ong, Walter J. 1982. *Orality and Literacy.* New York: Methuen.

Plato. 1956. *Phaedrus.* Trans. W. C. Helmbold and W. G. Rabinowitz. New York: Bobbs-Merrill.

Segal, Charles. 1989. "Song, Ritual, and Commemoration in Early Greek Poetry and Tragedy." *Oral Tradition* 3:330–59.

Skerrett, Joseph. 1985. "Recitation to the Griot: Storytelling and Learning in Toni Morrison's *Song of Solomon*." In *Conjuring: Black Women, Fiction, and Literary Tradition*, ed. Marjorie Pryse and Hortense J. Spillers, 192–202. Bloomington: Indiana University Press.

Smitherman, Geneva. 1977. *Talkin' and Testifyin'*. Detroit: Wayne State University Press.

Thomas, H. Nigel. 1988. *From Folklore to Fiction*. New York: Greenwood Press.

Yates, Frances A. 1966. *The Art of Memory*. Chicago: University of Chicago Press.

Zumthor, Paul. 1990. *Oral Poetry*. Trans. Kathryn Murphy-Judy. Minneapolis: University of Minnesota Press.

Call and Response: Voice, Community, and Dialogic Structures in Toni Morrison's *Song of Solomon*

MARILYN SANDERS MOBLEY

He wanted to hear the sound of his own voice.
— Toni Morrison, *Song of Solomon*

What is realized in the novel is the process of coming to know one's own language as it is perceived in someone else's language.
— Mikhail Bakhtin, "Discourse in the Novel"

SINCE its publication in 1977, *Song of Solomon* has most often been read as an initiation novel of mythic quest in which the male protagonist, Milkman Dead, must come to terms with his personal and collective history to achieve a sense of identity.[1] Traditionally, this perspective on the novel focuses on oppositional patterns of competition and resistance between Milkman and others, the self and community. Such thematic interpretations, even when they acknowledge the black community as a metaphorical chorus and situate this chorus in the African American oral tradition, tend to view it, nonetheless, as a monologic structure with which the hero must contend. Although other interpretations view the community as a complex structure, they focus on the visual images of self and other and attribute this complexity more to definitions of self based on the perceptions of others than on the endless network of voices within the community represented in the text. Cynthia Davis argues, for example, that all of Morrison's characters suffer the consequences of internalizing the "look" of the racial other by trying to live up to an external image.[2]

My discussion argues for a shift in focus and a closer examination of the concept of community in the novel to illuminate how the text deconstructs generally accepted, yet reductive notions of the black community as a single-voiced whole, at the same time that it reconstructs it as a dynamic, complex, multivoiced network of ongoing dialogues within which the hero could participate. By reading this text through the theoretical work of Henry Louis Gates Jr., Mikhail Bakhtin, Mae Henderson, Dale Bauer, and others, we can situate the locus of meaning in *Song of Solomon* on discourse and representations of voice. Thus, Milkman's initiation is not merely a matter of acquiring his own voice but one of recognizing that the relationship between the voice of the self and the voices of the community is not either/or but both/and. By extension, the relationship between the reader and the text is interactive and participatory. The spaces that Morrison creates in the text of *Song of Solomon* for her reader allow her or him to engage in a dialogue with both the text itself and the various dialogic structures embedded within it.³ By "dialogic structures" I mean those places in the text where the reader can hear multiple voices in dialogue or conversation with one another. At any given moment, the language points not to a single meaning but to diverse layers of meaning that grow out of African American culture and African American ways of knowing and speaking. Like Milkman, the reader learns to hear the dialogues and recognize the epistemological significance of multiple voices within the organization of identity and culture. This discussion offers a close reading of the text to uncover some of these dialogic structures and to suggest that they offer alternative possibilities for examining the narrative strategies, cultural resources, and political implications of Morrison's writing. Essentially, I argue that examining the concepts of voice and community in *Song of Solomon* enables us to recognize the dynamics at the heart of the cultural poetics in Morrison's writing: the desire to enact in fiction the processes by which African Americans routinely disrupt the power of the gaze or how others see them through the language they use to define themselves and to give voice to themselves as subjects rather than objects. More specifically, the novel challenges received notions of manhood that are based on the subjugation of women's voices. What *Song of Solomon* does ultimately is suggest that a viable sense of African American identity comes from responding to alternative constructions of self and community other than those received from mainstream American culture. / *Discuss*

1

It is probably no surprise that *Song of Solomon* is often read as a bildungsroman or initiation novel. Morrison's narrative rendering of the black community and her protagonist's problematic relationship with himself, his family, and that community all lend themselves to such readings. Some have focused on the resonances of classical myth that lie in the hero's struggle to come to terms with his familial past and the history of the community.[4] Others, such as Joseph Skerrett, have focused on the forms of black vernacular, such as wordplay, song, and storytelling, that appear as signs of the African American oral tradition and that function as a communal response to the hero's call.[5] Such readings have given us valuable points of departure for reading this text. The risk, however, is that these readings can produce interpretations that overlook the complex forms of dialogue that are embedded within the character of Milkman and beneath the surface configurations of community. Consequently, they inadvertently reduce the idea of community to a fixed, monologic entity − that is, to a single-voiced sameness − that the writer has simply represented mimetically in fiction.

Recent modes of inquiry in African American literary criticism, feminist criticism, cultural criticism, and literary criticism in general, however, offer us new critical directions into the text of *Song of Solomon*. We can thus begin to examine how and where African American modes of discourse shape this novel. Ultimately, we can deepen our notions of characterization to embrace more complex dialogic concepts of voice and identity, self and community, language and discourse. In other words, as Jonathan Culler, Gayatri Spivak, and Cheryl Wall have argued, respectively, we can read the novel not only to discover how previous readings were made possible but also to discover what these same readings overlooked about the relationship between the text and the cultural context it inscribes and of which it is a part.[6] Moreover, we can challenge the protagonist's reading of his own life and trace the epistemological journey he undertakes to come to a new understanding of himself in relation to others.

The shift from thematics and traditional modes of inquiry should not be interpreted as a retreat from hermeneutics or interpretation of the text. Instead, it should be interpreted as a means of connecting hermeneutics (*what* the text means) with poetics (*how* the text produces meaning) to enable the reader to hear, describe, and explain what Henry Louis Gates Jr. refers to as the "play of voices" and the dynamics of community that lie within the spaces of the text.[7] As Morrison herself says, *Song of Solomon* is full of spaces which

> were planned . . . [and] can conceivably be filled with other significances. . . . The point is that into these spaces should fall the ruminations of the reader and his or her invented or recollected or misunderstood knowingness. The reader as narrator asks the questions the community asks, and both reader and "voice" stand among the crowd, within it, with privileged intimacy and contact, but without any more privileged information than the crowd has.[8]

These spaces in the text are not unlike what Wolfgang Iser refers to as the "unseen joints of the text . . . [that] mark off schemata and textual perspectives from one another . . . [and that] simultaneously trigger acts of ideation . . . on the reader's part."[9] Calling attention to the play of voices within readers and in the novel enables the reader to speculate further about Morrison's narrative intentions and to discern the "other significances" of community that have never been fully explored and that derive not only from the text but from the various forms of cultural knowledge that her readers bring to the text.[10]

When it was published in 1977, *Song of Solomon* was a kind of literary intervention into what Morrison perceived to be a cultural crisis in the black community. For her, this crisis was the danger that black people might lose the rootedness the oral tradition had historically provided when the African American community was less geographically dispersed. She observes in "Rootedness: The Ancestor as Foundation":

> We don't live in places where we can hear those stories anymore; parents don't sit around and tell their children those classical, mythological archetypal stories that we heard years ago. But the new

information has got to get out, and there are several ways to do it. One is in the novel. . . . It should have the ability to be both print and oral literature . . . to make you stand up and . . . feel something profoundly in the same way that a black preacher requires his congregation to speak . . . to make that connection.[11]

Although it is clear that all of Morrison's novels privilege this oral quality, the distinct manifestations of voice in *Song of Solomon* make it exemplary of how the oral tradition, more commonly known in contemporary critical discourse as the vernacular, informs her representation of community.

"Voice" in the context of literary study traditionally refers to the authorial presence of the narrator. This presence or "point of view" is generally regarded as the controlling force throughout a work. My use of the term, however, is partly informed by the recent theoretical work of Henry Louis Gates Jr. and the rediscovered scholarship of Mikhail Bakhtin, both of whom challenge us to hear the multiplicity of voices and meanings that are latent in any given text. Gates, in particular, offers us new ways of reading and theorizing about African American texts that are pertinent to understanding how Morrison uses language in *Song of Solomon*. In *The Signifying Monkey: A Theory of Afro-American Literary Criticism*, for example, Gates reminds us that the black expressive tradition is "double-voiced." That is, it "operates between black vernacular discourse and standard English discourse."[12] Moreover, through his close reading of Zora Neale Hurston's *Their Eyes Were Watching God*, Gates identifies many of the complex modes of narration and signifying that characterize black vernacular discourse in black texts. This scholarship on the black vernacular not only reveals the intertextual relationship between Hurston and Morrison but provides a means of assessing how Morrison's use of the vernacular extends the cultural work of her literary precursor by problematizing and signifying on the notion of voice in *Song of Solomon*. If we understand signifying to mean black vernacular modes of rhetorical play that include the tropes of naming, boasting, innuendo, indirection, repetition, and creative revision, then Morrison's characterization of Milkman can be read as one that "signifies on" (that is, indirectly, but creatively, revises) Hurston's characterization of Janie Starks. In other words, while the focus of Hurston's novel is a black woman's quest for self and consciousness as a "speaking black subject," the focus of Morrison's novel is ostensibly a black man's growth into consciousness of himself as an individual, as one voice among the many other speaking black subjects of his community, at the same time that it is profoundly about the discursive process by which the African American community gives voice to itself, inscribes itself in language, and thereby resists the very cultural hegemony that has marginalized it.[13]

Bakhtin's *Dialogic Imagination,* especially the essay, "Discourse in the Novel," offers us other critical tools for rereading *Song of Solomon.* He suggests that voice is not only the obvious presence of the author's narrator but the various forms that narration might take in addition to the individualized speech of characters: "The novel orchestrates all its themes, the totality of the world of objects and ideas depicted and expressed in it, by means of the social diversity of speech types . . . and by differing individual voices that flourish under such conditions."[14] Consequently, we cannot read the novel as one monologue after another orchestrated solely by the author but must interpret it, instead, as a dialogized network of a "variety of links and interrelationships."[15] Although Bakhtin considers the novel the most dialogized of all literary forms, it is at the level of the utterance that he actually provides the best definition of dialogism. He explains that utterances "are aware of and mutually reflect one another. . . . Each utterance is filled with echoes and reverberations of other utterances to which it is related by the communality of the sphere of speech communication."[16]

In a dialogic reading of *Song of Solomon,* then, we have to pay attention to these interrelationships and signifying reverberations at nearly every point in the novel. By so doing, we discover that both direct and indirect discourse appear in the novel against a "background made up of contradictory opinions, points of view, value judgements."[17] Moreover, by drawing on recent feminist scholarship, we can speculate about the gendered discourse that also determines the interrelationships within the text. In other words, Gates's articulation of a black vernacular theory that examines the intertextual dynamics of racial discourse and Bakhtin's articulation of a sociolinguistic theory that exposes the dynamics of all novelistic discourse are inadequate without attention to how men's and women's voices are shaped by cultural constructions of masculine and feminine difference and how these constructions manifest themselves in identity formation.

The scholarship of Dale Bauer and Mae Henderson not only offers paradigms for examining male identity in relationship to women but extends our understandings of voice and power relations in community. For example, Dale Bauer's *Feminist Dialogics: A Theory of Failed Community* reveals that when we add gender considerations to Bakhtin's literary stylistics, we can examine how interpretive communities silence women's voices as well as other voices deemed subversive or resistant to the dominant social order.[18] Moreover, Mae Henderson's theory of the "simultaneity of discourse," which argues that race and gender are always mutually interdependent discursive approaches to black women writers' texts, offers us an interpretive strategy for foregrounding this interconnection, for reading Milkman's character in relationship to his African American identity and his connection to women.[19] Finally, the work of Valerie Smith and Sandra Zagarell, who identify *Song of Solomon* as a narrative of community, gives us a way of naming Morrison's poetics and of describing alternative strategies for reading the novel. Asserting that a communal sense of identity informs the novel, Smith explains that Milkman's task is to learn that "identity is a collective rather than an individual construct."[20] Zagarell goes a step further by identifying "narrative of community" as a distinct genre that represents women's "response to [the] cultural-historical circumstances" of their lives and thus offers an interpretive strategy that reveals the dialogic connection between voice and community that gives form and meaning to *Song of Solomon*. Of particular value is Zagarell's discussion of the connection between gender and genre which shows how women's texts deconstruct monolithic, individualistic notions of self and depict interdependent multivoiced communities at the same time that they stylistically shift from linear to cyclical, more process-oriented narrative strategies.[21] All these theoretical perspectives are congenial to this discussion of *Song of Solomon* and, indeed, to other African American texts, because they offer ways of naming what Gates refers to as "indigenous black principles of criticism," principles which are inherent in Morrison's rendering of black expressive discourse in the novel.[22]

2

As the foregoing discussion indicates, my critical approach to *Song of Solomon* is actually a rereading of the novel reminiscent of what Adrienne Rich calls "re-vision" – that is, "the act of looking back, of seeing with fresh eyes, of entering an old text from a new critical direction."[23] I am arguing here, however, that one way to (re)enter *Song of Solomon* is to hear the text with fresh ears, to listen to the multiple voices that give the community Morrison creates its unique identity, for this is the very process that Milkman must undertake to achieve a sense of his identity. As Michel Foucault asserts:

> The frontiers of a book are never clear-cut: beyond the title, the first lines, and the last full stop, beyond its internal configurations and its autonomous form, it is caught up in a system of references to other books, other texts, other sentences: it is a node within a network. . . . The book . . . indicates itself, constructs itself, only on the basis of a complex field of discourse.[24]

In other words, in taking my cues from the African American vernacular tradition and from a gendered understanding of that tradition, my interpretation of the text does not privilege the eye or the power of the Western hegemonic gaze (inscribed in critical discourse by the focus on images – that is, visual perceptions and representations of the other) but instead focuses on voice (with all its attendant signifying powers to subvert the dominant forces of the gaze). In shifting from the gaze and the specular to the oral and the aural, we begin to hear some of the complex structures of African American discourse by which black people resist oppression.[25] Thus, Morrison participates in the larger cultural project that Abdul JanMohamed argues is characteristic of minority discourse; that is, it attempts "to negate the prior hegemonic negation of itself . . . [as] one of its most fundamental forms of affirmation," at the same time that it critiques cultural hegemony.[26] But

before I attend to the voices and the dialogic structures they inscribe, it might be useful to summarize, if only briefly, the plot of
this long and structurally complex novel.

Song of Solomon is divided into two parts. In Part I, the protagonist, Macon Dead III, is, in 1931, the first black baby ever born in
Mercy Hospital, a hospital the black community has appropriately
renamed No Mercy Hospital. He is born the day after Mr. Smith,
an insurance agent, attempts "to fly from Mercy to the other side
of Lake Superior" (3). He acquires the name Milkman when it is
learned that his mother is still nursing him long past the time it is
considered normal to do so. His father, Macon Dead II, is a cold,
insensitive, materially defined man who uses his position and authority as a wealthy "propertied" man, not only to intimidate his
tenants, who regard him as a slum landlord, but to intimidate his
wife, Ruth, his daughters, Lena and First Corinthians, and even
Milkman. Macon forbids Milkman to visit his Aunt Pilate because
he is embarrassed by her eccentric ways, her unkempt appearance,
and her stubborn persistence in making bootleg wine. In Macon's
words to Milkman:

> Pilate can't teach you a thing you can use in this world. Maybe the
> next, but not this one. Let me tell you right now the one important
> thing you'll ever need to know: Own things. And let the things you
> own own other things. Then you'll own yourself and other people
> too. (55)

Frustrated with his loveless, emotionally and spiritually "dead"
family, bored with his unfulfilling sex life with Hagar, his cousin,
and fundamentally dissatisfied with life in general, he gives up his
middle-class comforts and heads south in search of the gold inheritance his father has told him about.

Part II traces Milkman's journey through the South, a journey
transformed from a search for gold to a quest to learn the meaning
of a song he had heard Pilate sing at home in Michigan. He learns
that the song encodes his family history, including the story of
Solomon, his paternal great-grandfather, who, according to the
story in the song, flew away from slavery back to Africa. Milkman's
quest also includes forays into communal storytelling; a visit to
Circe, the midwife who delivered his father and aunt; and the

male ritual of hunting. Upon discovering that the alleged bag of gold he sought is actually a sack containing the bones of his grandfather, he escorts Pilate to the South and helps her give her father a proper burial. As she dies in his arms, he sings the song he had once regarded as a nonsense nursery rhyme and discovers that like his flying ancestor, he too has the power of flight, which proved that "[i]f you surrendered to the air, you could *ride* it" (337). Although this synopsis establishes some of the rich texture of the plot, there is much more going on within the spaces of the novel. Of the various manifestations of voice that participate in the interplay of voices in *Song of Solomon,* I would like to name three – the narrative voice, the signifying voice, and the responsive voice – each of which is dialogized within itself and in relation to the others.

In the opening scene of the novel, the third-person omniscient narrative voice informs us that at the time of day that Mr. Smith plans to fly from the roof of Mercy Hospital, "word-of-mouth news just lumbered along" (3). This phrase not only encodes the black vernacular but also immediately directs the reader's attention to the cultural, communicative process by which the community structures itself. Interestingly, the phrase appears in the second sentence after Mr. Smith's note about his planned flight appears in the text. Thus, it abruptly shifts the reader's attention from the spectacle of Mr. Smith to the linguistic community of which he is a part. For this community, word of mouth is both a mode of communication and a category of knowledge upon which its members depend. The phrase also stands in contrast to the written word of Mr. Smith's note and therefore, paradoxically, points to his announcement as a suspension of the normative, just as the description of the community that follows the phrase suspends the reader, along with the curious crowd of onlookers. On the one hand, the narrative voice contextualizes the act of an individual with the attendant communal response; on the other hand, it concurrently informs the reader and abdicates any totalizing ability to do so.

Perhaps more importantly, however, in the litany of information about how the black community names Mains Avenue "Not Doctor Street" and names Mercy Hospital "No Mercy Hospital," Morrison gives voices to the community and illustrates how it uses this

"word-of-mouth" communication to challenge municipal authorities, to critique and resist their racist practices, and to assert their
own identity all at once. Thus, their act of negation is simultaneously a critique of racist politics and an affirmation of their
ability to resist these politics through the power of the word,
through their collective voice. All of this information prepares the
reader for the significance of Milkman's birth at the hospital that
had previously had a whites-only policy. To read this phrase dialogically then, is to hear it in the context of the heteroglossic
historical, cultural, and political voices that create it.[27] The narrative voice creates distance at the same time that it is infused with
the same everyday language – the vernacular – that it foregrounds
through the voices of the characters in the crowd.

But within this crowd is Pilate, who is initially introduced as the
"woman who suddenly burst into song" (5). Her voice not only
disrupts the gaze of the crowd at the spectacle of Mr. Smith, who is
poised for flight, but also introduces her as an alternative narrative
voice, whose story in the song prompts the crowd to listen "as
though it were the helpful and defining piano music in a silent
movie" (6). At this early point in the novel, however, the reader
has no way of knowing that this song will become the narrative
thread of the novel. It is only near the end of the novel that we
know the narrator in the song is, not one, but many, that it is, not
one voice that sings of this flight, but a chorus of voices. The four
lines of the song that are presented at this point seem both parodic
and disruptive. They do not really clarify anything for the reader or
the crowd but instead foreground the vernacular, this time through
the grammatical construction and rhythm of the blues song:

> O Sugarman done fly away
> Sugarman done gone
> Sugarman cut across the sky
> Sugarman gone home. . . . (6)

The words of the song seem to inform (indicate a connection
between the anticipated "flight" of the insurance man and the
legendary flight of an African ancestor) and withhold information
from the crowd and the reader at one and the same time. Nevertheless, the sniggering response of some and the silent listening

of others suggest the crowd's acceptance of Pilate's voice and presence. What the reader bears witness to is the process by which community is created out of the context of shared experience.

But the characterization of Macon Dead II represents a form of disruption that is less acceptable. His easy assimilation into the worst extremes of capitalistic acquisition, greed, and power cause him to silence others – with physical force, in the case of his wife, with intimidation, in the case of his children, and with the threat of eviction, in the case of his tenants. It can be argued that in the introduction of his character, the narrative voice operates through formal literary language, exacting verbs, and vivid imagery to emphasize how his oppressive form of male domination constrains voice and attempts to silence those who would resist it:

> Solid, rumbling, likely to erupt without prior notice, Macon kept each member of his family awkward with fear. His hatred of his wife glittered and sparked in every word he spoke to her. The disappointment he felt in his daughters sifted down on them like ash, dulling their buttery complexions and choking the lilt out of what should have been girlish voices. Under the frozen heat of his glance they tripped over doorsills and dropped the salt cellar into the yolks of their poached eggs. The way he mangled their grace, wit, and self-esteem was the single excitement of their days. . . . [H]is wife, Ruth, began her days stunned into stillness by her husband's contempt and ended them wholly animated by it. (10–11)

Like the oxymoronic phrase "frozen heat," this passage is rife with the contradictory conditions that Macon creates with his presence. The passage reveals at once the oppressive noise of male patriarchal domination and the equally oppressive "sound" of the female silence produced by the male gaze of contempt. In place of the "girlish voices" that have been snuffed out is the implied inner discourse of female desire. Moreover, the description of Ruth's obsessive need to look at a water mark left on the dining table where there once had been a bowl for floral arrangements suggests the very different form of inner discourse that is going on within her. The water mark assures her that "she was alive somewhere, inside, which she acknowledged to be true only because a thing she knew intimately was out there, outside herself" (11). Thus, the narrative voice allows the reader not only to hear the sound of male domination but also to hear the response to it and the consequences of it for the female voice.

But the narrative voice does more than inform the reader that Macon is an emotionally abusive father and that his marriage to Ruth is less than ideal. The narrative voice also illustrates how language, within this nuclear family, is stratified into at least three categories: the authoritative discourse of the father, the "silent" discourse of the mother, and the internally persuasive discourse of each child, but especially that of Milkman, whose gradual understanding of language the novel enacts.[28] We come to know Milkman through his responses to his father's oppressive voice and to his mother's repressed voice and through the inner dialogue that develops between these external voices and the voice that is in the process of becoming his own. Two separate scenes in the novel illustrate this process. One occurs when Milkman is twelve; the other, when he is twenty-two. In the first incident, which takes place in Chapter 2, Macon learns through Freddie, the town gossip, that Milkman has been seen drinking wine at Pilate's house. In the confrontation that ensues between father and son over Milkman's failure to obey Macon's strict order not to visit Pilate, Milkman asks why such visits are forbidden. Arguing that he owes him no explanation, Macon asserts: "As long as your feet are under my table, you'll do in this house what you are told" (50). When Milkman retorts that Macon is treating him "like a baby," Macon responds: "Don't raise your voice to me," followed by the injunction, "Watch your mouth" (50). This confrontation not only illustrates how Macon exercises parental control through language, which Jane Gallop says is "our inscription into patriarchy," but also represents Milkman's failed attempt to enter into that symbolic order through his own voice.[29]

In the second incident, which occurs in Chapter 3, when Milkman is a twenty-two-year-old adult, he is more successful in challenging his father's authority. In the description of how a seemingly harmless dinner conversation erupts into a verbal and then physical struggle, the narrative voice not only complicates the dynamics of the Dead household but establishes the emotionally charged discursive context from which Milkman seeks to liberate himself. When Macon raises his hand to strike Ruth a second time for having the audacity to challenge him verbally, Milkman's threat "You touch her again, one more time, and I'll kill you" has the effect of making Macon "so shocked at being assaulted he could not speak" (67). The shift in power relations that this family altercation creates illustrates the validity of Dale Bauer's assertion that "each internalization of repression contains the possibility of rebellion."[30] Indeed, by raising their voices against Macon's patriarchal domination, both Ruth and Milkman disrupt the established order that has operated by silencing them.

Yet, although he successfully averts the violence against his mother, he is less successful in coming to terms with the implications of raising his voice to undermine his father's authority. The dialogic nature of his inner discourse reveals both the power of patriarchal domination and the equally powerful desire to resist its control. Milkman feels "his own contradictions" at the same time that he feels "glee" that he "had won something and lost something in the same instant" (68). Yet his words create a combination of "infinite possibilities and enormous responsibilities" (67) that ultimately overwhelm him. In the process of winning a temporary victory over his father, he loses his ideal image of him. Moreover, what the reader notices is the indeterminacy of separating Macon's voice from Milkman's, for in Milkman's threat to Macon — "I'll kill you" — we hear the language (authoritative discourse) he has learned (that is, internalized) from his father. Moments later, when he goes to his room and gazes at his own reflection in the mirror, he discovers "it lacked coherence, a coming together of the features into a total self" (69). According to Jacques Lacan, the mirror stage of childhood "situates the agency of the ego, before its social determination, in a fictional direction, which will always remain irreducible for the individual alone."[31] What the novel enacts then, through the narrative voice, is the process that Milkman, who "had stretched his carefree boyhood out for thirty-one years" (98), must undergo to wrest himself from his fictional self — that is, from the gaze of his own reflection and the incoherent sound of his own voice — to comprehend the interconnection between self and other generally, and specifically between himself and the voices he has learned to repress through the internalization of his father's authoritative discourse. Although Milkman undervalues or marginalizes the male voices of his community, it is the female voices that he represses. Thus, Morrison suggests in *Song of Solomon* that male individuation involves more than the rejection of patriarchal domination; it also requires the recognition of one's inscription into patriarchal discourse as well as one's connection to the female voices that that discourse represses in our culture. Jessica Benjamin refers to this form of mutual recognition as intersubjectivity, a recognition of other speaking subjects as both like and different from oneself.[32] Through the third-person narrative voice the novel both orchestrates all of these dialogic elements and reveals how they complicate Milkman's growth into an intersubjective consciousness.

Whereas the narrative voice introduces the individuation process and the cultural, ideological context of language operating in the Dead family, it is through the signifying voice that the reader hears the implications of this process for Milkman's voice as he interacts in the community outside his family. Drawing on the vernacular theory of signifying developed by Gates, I define the signifying voice as the double-voiced mode of discourse in the text based on African American rhetorical strategies of repetition, the play of difference, insult, naming, indirection, circumlocution, "loud-talking, testifying, calling out (of one's name), sounding, rapping, playing the dozens, and so on."[33] Although there are instances of female characters who speak in the signifying voice, it appears most often in *Song of Solomon* in male discourse at predominantly male gatherings. The importance of this voice is not only that it reveals the play of multiple voices in dialogue with one another within the African American community but that it reveals Milkman's alienation from his own voice and his inability to hear his connection to the language of others. In other words, the intertextual relationship between his discourse and theirs eludes him.

One of the best examples of the signifying voice appears in Railroad Tommy's Barbershop, where Milkman is an outsider to the ritualistic swapping of stories, name-calling, and verbal banter in which most of the other men are engaged. In the words of the text, Milkman tries to "focus on the crisscrossed conversations"

(80). The fact that the dialogue seems "crisscrossed" to him emphasizes his status not only as an outsider to his own gender group but as an outsider to the collective knowledge inscribed in its discourse. Moreover, because he is self-absorbed, he attempts to "focus on" – that is, "see" – their discourse rather than actively listen to and participate in it. While one mode of experience – seeing – reifies the boundaries between self and other, the other mode – hearing – facilitates the intersubjective growth into consciousness by both establishing boundaries and blurring them. As the men listen to the news on the radio about the murder of Emmett Till, their dialogue begins:

> "It'll be in the morning paper."
> "Maybe it will, and maybe it won't," said Porter.
> "It was on the radio! Got to be in the paper!" said Freddie.
> "They don't put that kind of news in no white paper. Not unless he raped somebody." (80)

In this exchange, Morrison gives voice to more than what we literally read or hear. She gives voice to black vernacular speech, to differences of opinion, to communal knowledge of how racism and sexism operate in America, to communal speculation, to collective memories, and to historical realities within the community. Moreover, the speaker who signifies on the term "news" by implicating the selectivity of the white-controlled print media illustrates his knowledge of the politics of language and race.

Thus, a kind of multiple signifying occurs. As author, Morrison signifies on the novel as a fictional genre by incorporating the historical allusion to the 1955 murder of Emmett Till, an act of racism that ignited racial tensions in the North and South, and by blurring the boundaries between fact and fiction.[34] She further signifies on the injustice of this historical event deeply ingrained in African American cultural memory by imagining a group – the Seven Days – that avenges such acts within the community created in the novel. In a sense, the historical allusion has an intertextual connection to Richard Wright's character Bigger Thomas, whose murder of his girlfriend, Bessie, in the novel *Native Son*, elicits no response in comparison to the outcry over the murder of Mary Dalton, the daughter of the wealthy white family for whom he worked. The allusions not only open up discourse in the novel but indicate that the text contains an endless play of signifiers that preclude the possibility of closure and that allow us to hear a multiplicity of voices, interpretations, and intertextual echoes.[35]

In addition, the narrative voice signifies – that is, implicitly comments on – Milkman's cultural/linguistic ignorance and naivete by drawing attention to his position outside the conversation as an observer rather than a participant. The men signify on one another and on the hegemonic media that make distinctions about what is newsworthy along racial lines. In a sense, they engage in a form of metalinguistic signifying: they use language to talk about how others misuse language to marginalize them. Milkman's preoccupation with himself, and his inscription, despite his efforts to resist, into his father's either/or thinking and bourgeois values, cause him to discount the men's barbershop talk, not to hear the various levels of meaning embedded in it, and ultimately to feel just as alienated from them as he does from his father. Thus, the signifying voice not only illustrates male constructions of identity in the African American community but reveals and critiques Milkman's estrangements both from that community and from his own voice.

Although I have stratified these voices and their functions for purposes of illustration and clarification, none is mutually exclusive in actuality, because they are all dialogized and contain echoes and reverberations of one another within themselves. If the narrative voice primarily informs, and the signifying voice primarily critiques, then the responsive voice completes the dialogic interaction between the speaker and the listener. In a sense, however, the responsive voice is the larger context from which the signifying voice is derived. It requires the active participation of speaker and listener, just as the signifying voice enables both the speaker and the listener to exchange roles and become speaking subjects. Perhaps the best definition of the responsive voice can be found in the definition of the African American vernacular tradition of call and response, which Geneva Smitherman defines as an African-derived communication process of "spontaneous verbal and nonverbal interaction between speaker and listener in which all of the speaker's statements ('calls') are punctuated by expressions ('responses') from the listener."[36] The signs of the responsive voice in

Song of Solomon, then, are those places in the text where Morrison enacts this communication process and thereby illustrates the cultural/linguistic dynamics through which the community operates. I am not, however, merely grafting Bakhtinian dialogism onto vernacular discourse in this text. Instead, I am arguing that dialogism, as Bakhtin theorizes it, is indigenous to the African American expressive tradition. The concept of dialogism enables us to place shared ways of knowing, interpreting, and speaking at the center of any discussion about the African American community. At the same time it enables us to hear the diverse multiplicity of voices that are always already at work within African American discourse.

The reader recognizes the responsive voice, more specifically, at those places in *Song of Solomon* where a character is both aware of his or her own voice and also able to hear, actively listen to, and participate in dialogue with another. It is that voice that affirms the intersubjectivity or interconnectedness between speaking subjects. For example, the conversations in the barbershop illustrate the responsive voice at work in the community of men. Earlier in the novel, near the end of Chapter 1, in the scene where Pilate, Reba, and Hagar participate in a form of choral singing, we have an example of the responsive voice in a community of women:

> They were singing some melody that Pilate was leading. A phrase that the other two were taking up and building on. Her powerful contralto, Reba's piercing soprano in counterpoint, and the soft voice of the girl, Hagar . . . (29)

Each voice both responds to and sings in concert with the others. The focus is not on the individual sound of one but on the collective sound of all three voices in concert. This enactment of the call-and-response tradition illustrates, then, how the responsive voice fosters intersubjectivity and creates community in the context of shared experience.

Ironically, through this same scene the failure of community is signaled by a resistance to the call that anticipates the responsive voice. In this scene, Macon heads for home after work between dusk and twilight. At that time of evening, his houses "did not seem to belong to him at all – in fact he felt as though the houses were in league with one another to make him feel like the outsider, the propertyless, landless wanderer" (27). The text goes on to say it is this feeling of loneliness that prompts him to take a shortcut into that part of town where Pilate lives. As he approaches her house, he hears the music of their singing. Macon first walks on "resisting as best he could the sound of the voices that followed him" (28). Yet their voices "pulled him like a carpet tack under the influence of a magnet" (29):

> Surrendering to the sound, Macon moved closer. He wanted no conversation, no witness, only to listen and perhaps to see the three of them, the source of that music that made him think of fields and wild turkey and calico. . . . Near the window, hidden by the dark, he felt the irritability of the day drain from him and relished the effortless beauty of the women singing in the candlelight. . . . As Macon felt himself softening under the weight of memory and music, the song died down. . . . He liked looking at them freely this way. (29–30)

Here, Macon consciously resists the responsive voice within his own voice that would connect him with this community of women. Moreover, by choosing to remain invisible to them, he maintains the delusion of his own individual autonomy of self at the same time that the reader recognizes his dependence on others. Despite his continual attempts to repress Pilate's voice by forbidding Milkman to see her, in this scene, he secretly indulges his own need to see her. By so doing, he reveals his need to distance himself from the other as woman by objectifying her under the male gaze. His voyeuristic gaze allows him to maintain the facade of the self-sufficient man who maintains, at all cost, the separation between autonomy and attachment, nurturance and self-sufficiency.[37] Thus, although Macon hears their singing, he fails to listen actively by participating with them, by acknowledging them or allowing them to acknowledge him. Instead of reentering the community symbolized by this triad of women and the context of shared experiences he remembers, he attempts once again to maintain his sense of privilege and control over others. What we have in this scene, then, is an example of what Kaja Silverman calls "the acoustic mirror," in which Macon is ambivalently drawn to the sight and sound of the very female voice he has so stridently repressed.[38]

In a later scene in the novel, through the characterization of Milkman, Morrison deconstructs notions of manhood predicated on illusions of self-sufficiency and on the repression of other voices, especially the voices of marginalized subjects (in this case, women, tenants, children, and so on). Through an enactment of the responsive voice, Morrison celebrates Milkman's ability to engage in active listening, to move out of his narcissistic self long enough to be able to hear another's voice, and suggests that this ability is in sharp contrast to his father's inability to move outside the strictures of patriarchal domination. Drawing on the black vernacular tradition of call and response that informs African American music, storytelling, and verbal communication, Morrison enacts how the process of call and response operates to connect speaker and listener. Milkman overhears school children singing and

> their sweet voices reminded him of the gap in his own childhood. . . . The boy in the middle of the circle . . . spun around . . . until the song ended with a shout. . . . Then they all [began] another song. . . . That old blues song Pilate sang all the time: "O Sugarman don't leave me here," except the children sang, "Solomon don't leave me here."
> . . . These children were singing a story about his own people! (300, 304)

The voices of these children not only evoke childhood memories but embody two African American vernacular traditions at once: storytelling and the blues. Indeed, the words of the song appear throughout the text as a kind of recurring frame story that punctuates the text with these two traditions and with the voices from the past that were embedded within the song. Moreover, because the song evokes the memory of Pilate as singer and storyteller, it reconstructs her not as the crazy woman Macon would have him believe her to be but as the griot figure – the African ancestral storyteller that she was.[39] In fact, when he suddenly realizes that there is meaning in the song, he decides to write down the words as the children continue to sing. Having neither pen nor pencil he realizes he "would just have to listen and memorize it" (303). As the voices of the children evoke memories and meaning, he is drawn into the community of shared experience and into his own family history. He discovers, in essence, that Pilate has been teaching him all his life who he was/is/could be. Ironically, the fact that Milkman comes to value Pilate, the very person Macon privately watches and listens to but publicly seeks to repress and denigrate, illustrates Bauer's feminist dialogical principle that "language is not just a prison house; it . . . produces occasions for its own disruption and critique."⁴⁰ In other words, within the very song and voices Milkman had denigrated were the words which would disrupt his learned attempt to objectify others and their words as irrelevant to his existence.

Thus, Milkman learns to respond to the very voices he had been conditioned to ignore under the discipline of patriarchal hegemony. Contrary to what his father tells him, Pilate not only teaches him something he can use – as much of his heritage and identity as it is within her capacity to share – but also helps him understand the near uselessness of his father's selfish materialism. Her song teaches the truth of what his friend, Guitar, tries to tell him: "Wanna fly, you got to give up the shit that weighs you down" (179). Pilate's song and the children's song become one at the same time that they comment on one another and engage in dialogue with one another to connect young and old, familiar and unfamiliar, past and present, present and future. In part, the novel enacts the process, therefore, by which Milkman gives up the individualism that weighs him down and comes to understand the connection between language, identity, and community.

3

A dialogic reading of *Song of Solomon* has value beyond that of offering revisionary interpretations of the novel, in general, or of the male protagonist, in particular. As Deborah E. McDowell argues, it has implications for the reading process itself.⁴¹ It enables us to read beyond the signs in the text to hear the voices and ideologies embedded within those signs. It also calls attention to the relationship between the text and the reader, a relationship that reiterates Morrison's own narrative intentions. As she asserts:

There are things that I try to incorporate into my fiction that are directly and deliberately related to what I regard as Black art, wherever it is. One of which is the ability to be both print and oral literature: to combine those two aspects so that the stories can be read in silence, of course, but one should be able to hear them as well. . . . In the same way that a musician's music is enhanced when there is a response from the audience . . . to have the reader work *with* the author in the construction of the book – is what's important. . . . To construct the dialogue so that it is heard.[42]

In reading dialogically, the reader gains an appreciation for the said and participates in the dialogue of the text by giving voice – that is, by "hearing" – the unsaid. In other words, the reader must "listen" to the text and respond if what Bakhtin calls the "chain of speech communion" is to remain unbroken.[43] Although it is impossible to account fully for the process by which the reader responds, my reading of Milkman's epistemological journey from ignorance to knowledge suggests that voice evokes memory, which in turn produces meaning. Just as Milkman's listening to his ancestral song evokes memories which in turn produce both knowledge and meaning, so too does the reader's "listening" to the text evoke memories that draw him or her into the meanings of the text. In other words, out of the context of memory or shared experience, what is heard takes on significance to the listener.

By paying attention to how identity is constructed dialogically rather than monologically, the reader hears and celebrates the voices that Toni Morrison both directly and indirectly enacts in the text. But this process also enables the reader to critique those cultural hegemonic forces that have silenced some voices in the first place. A dialogic reading not only encourages the reader to relinquish interpretations which reduce the African American community to a monologic, manageable entity but discourages the reader from coming to closure too easily. As Henderson explains, "[B]lack women, speaking out of the specificity of their racial and gender experiences, are able to communicate in a diversity of discourses."[44] As a black woman writer's text, *Song of Solomon* thrives on the endless play of meanings in the vernacular, on the intersubjective relationship between speaking subjects, and on the notion of identity as a matter of process or becoming rather than as stasis. By privileging voice over vision, sound over sight, and hearing over seeing, this novel illustrates the ways in which our current cultural moment is engaged in what James Clifford refers to as a rejection of the "visualism" privileged in Western literate cultures. The focus is therefore, as he argues, on "a cultural poetics that is an interplay of voices, of positioned utterances. In a discursive rather than a visual paradigm, the dominant metaphors . . . shift away from the observing eye and toward expressive speech."⁴⁵ Finally, a dialogic reading of *Song of Solomon* encourages us to question Western notions of autonomy and individuality as the white male constructions that they are, and to consider, instead, how revised notions of community offer us new ways to read black texts and new ways to hear and respond to the multivocality that has made us who we are and who we are becoming.

NOTES

1. For discussions of the novel as bildungsroman, initiation narrative, and mythic quest, see Leslie A. Harris, "Myth as Structure in Toni Morrison's *Song of Solomon*," *MELUS* 17 (1980): 69–82; Wilfred D. Samuels, "Liminality and the Search for Self in Toni Morrison's *Song of Solomon*," *Minority Voices* (1981): 59–68; Cynthia A. Davis, "Self, Society, and Myth in Toni Morrison's Fiction," *Contemporary Literature* 23 (Summer 1982): 333–42; Valerie Smith, "The Quest for and Discovery of Identity in Toni Morrison's *Song of Solomon*," *Southern Review* 21 (Summer 1985): 721–32; Gerry Brenner, "*Song of Solomon*: Rejecting Rank's Monomyth and Feminism," in *Critical Essays on Toni Morrison*, ed. Nellie Y. McKay (Boston: G. K. Hall, 1988), 114–25; and Marilyn Sanders Mobley, *Folk Roots and Mythic Wings in Sarah Orne Jewett and Toni Morrison: The Cultural Function of Narrative* (Baton Rouge: Louisiana State University Press, 1991). The epigraphs are taken from Toni Morrison, *Song of Solomon* (New York: Knopf, 1977), 214; and Mikhail Bakhtin, "Discourse in the Novel," in *The Dialogic Imagination: Four Essays by M. M. Bakhtin*, trans. Caryl Emerson and Michael Holquist, ed. Michael Holquist (Austin: University of Texas Press, 1981), 365. All subsequent references to *Song of Solomon* are cited in the text parenthetically.

I would like to express my appreciation to the National Endowment for the Humanities for their generous support of my early work on this article in the form of a 1989 Summer Stipend. I am also indebted to the National Research Council for a Ford Foundation Postdoctoral Fellowship (1989–90) and to George Mason University, whose support made it possible for me to expand my original essay into a chapter for my forthcoming study of cultural poetics in Morrison's fiction. I especially thank Claudia Tate, Jennifer Jordan, Victoria Arana Robinson, and Ann Kelly, members of the First Draft Club, for being such careful readers, superb critics, and supportive sisters/friends during the revising process. Finally, I thank Linda Williamson-Nelson, Cynthia Fuchs, and Devon Hodges for their suggestions for revising this essay.

2. See Kathleen O'Shaughnessy, " 'Life Life Life Life': The Community as Chorus in *Song of Solomon*," in McKay, ed., *Critical Essays*, 125–33; Susan L. Blake, "Folklore and Community in *Song of Solomon*," *MELUS* 7 (1980): 77–82; and Davis, "Self, Society, and Myth."

3. See Claudia Tate, "Toni Morrison," in *Black Women Writers at Work* (New York: Continuum, 1984), 125, for Morrison's comments on her desire to leave "spaces so that the reader can come into" her writing.

4. See Davis, "Self, Society, and Myth," 336. Also see Jane Campbell, "Ancestral Quests in Toni Morrison's *Song of Solomon* and David Bradley's *The Chaneysville Incident*," in *Mythic Black Fiction* (Knoxville: University of Tennessee Press, 1986), 136–53.

5. Joseph T. Skerrett, "Recitation to the Griot: Storytelling and Learning in Toni Morrison's *Song of Solomon*," in *Conjuring: Black Women, Fiction, and Literary Tradition*, ed. Marjorie Pryse and Hortense J. Spillers (Bloomington: Indiana University Press, 1985), 192–202.

6. See Jonathan Culler, *The Pursuit of Signs* (Ithaca: Cornell University Press, 1981); Gayatri Chakravorty Spivak, "Reading the World: Literary Studies in the Eighties," in *In Other Worlds: Essays in Cultural Politics* (New York: Methuen Books, 1987); and Cheryl Wall, "Taking Positions and Changing Words," in *Changing Our Own Words: Essays on Criticism, Theory, and Writing by Black Women*, ed. Cheryl Wall (New Brunswick: Rutgers University Press, 1989), 1–15. There are two studies that have begun this kind of contextual scholarship. Susan Willis suggests how we can move beyond the more obvious approaches to community in Morrison's fiction to understand the disturbing questions that complicate her novels. Wahneema Lubiano undertakes the even more difficult challenge of metacritical discourse to expose some of the limitations of previous readings of *Song of Solomon* and also to illuminate how the text itself calls some of those readings into question. My reading of the novel extends the project of

both of these studies. See Susan Willis, *Specifying: Black Women Writing the American Experience* (Madison: University of Wisconsin Press, 1987), and Wahneema Lubiano, "Messing with the Machine: Four Afro-American Novels and the Nexus of Vernacular, Historical Restraint and Narrative Strategy" (Ph.D. diss., Stanford University, 1987).

7. Henry Louis Gates Jr., *The Signifying Monkey: A Theory of Afro-American Literary Criticism* (New York: Oxford University Press, 1988), xxv.

8. Toni Morrison, "Unspeakable Things Unspoken: The Afro-American Presence in American Literature," *Michigan Quarterly Review* 28 (Winter 1989): 29.

9. Wolfgang Iser, *The Act of Reading: A Theory of Aesthetic Response* (Baltimore: Johns Hopkins University Press, 1978), 182–3.

10. By "cultural knowledge," I mean both the body of information and the ways of knowing that a reader brings to a given text. As members of interpretive communities, readers bring gendered positions; personal biases, assumptions, histories, memories, and ideologies; and received notions of others to their reading. All of these preclude claims of objectivity. What readers know or believe or do not know or believe about a given culture shapes their reading and interpretation of a text about that culture. As James Clifford asserts in the introduction to *Writing Culture: The Poetics and Politics of Ethnography* (Berkeley and Los Angeles: University of California Press, 1986), "No one reads from a neutral or final position" (18).

11. Toni Morrison, "Rootedness: The Ancestor as Foundation," in *Black Women Writers (1950–1980): A Critical Evaluation*, ed. Mari Evans (New York: Doubleday, Anchor Books, 1984), 340. The idea of the novel as both political and literary intervention is one I borrow from Hazel Carby, who argues that the emergence of African American women novelists must be viewed in the context of the "social formations in which they lived." See Hazel V. Carby, *Reconstructing Womanhood: The Emergence of the Afro-American Woman Novelist* (New York: Oxford University Press, 1987), 7.

12. Gates, *Signifying Monkey*, 50.

13. Ibid., 181. For an extensive review of the scholarship by Geneva Smitherman, Roger Abrahams, and others about the meanings and uses of signifying, see ibid., 52–88.

14. Bakhtin, "Discourse in the Novel," 263.

15. Ibid.

16. M. M. Bakhtin, "The Problem of Speech Genres," in *Speech Genres and*

Other Late Essays, trans. Vern W. McGee, ed. Caryl Emerson and Michael Holquist (Austin: University of Texas Press, 1986), 91.

17. Bakhtin, "Discourse in the Novel," 281.

18. Dale Bauer, *Feminist Dialogics: A Theory of Failed Community* (Albany: State University of New York Press, 1988).

19. Mae Henderson, "Speaking in Tongues: Dialogics, Dialectics, and the Black Woman Writer's Literary Tradition," in Wall, ed., *Changing Our Own Words,* 17.

20. Valerie Smith, *Self-Discovery and Authority in Afro-American Narrative* (Cambridge: Harvard University Press, 1987), 136.

21. Sandra A. Zagarell, "Narratives of Community: The Identification of a Genre," *SIGNS* 13 (Spring 1988): 502, 513.

22. See Henry Louis Gates Jr., "Authority, (White) Power and the (Black) Critic," *Cultural Critique* 7 (Fall 1987): 33.

23. Adrienne Rich, "When We Dead Awaken: Writing as Re-vision," *College English* 34 (October 1972): 18.

24. Michel Foucault, *The Archaeology of Knowledge and the Discourse on Language* (New York: Pantheon, 1972), 23.

25. In arguing for the value of focusing on voice rather than the gaze, I am contributing to the discussion Bauer undertakes in *Feminist Dialogics* by applying her adaptation of Bakhtin to a black woman's text to reveal in specific terms how both gender and race determine the play of voices in Morrison's novel and to how this play of voices subverts the very forces of patriarchal domination that have marginalized the African American community. See Bauer, *Feminist Dialogics,* xiii, and Nelly Furman, "The Politics of Language: Beyond the Gender Principle?" in *Making a Difference: Feminist Literary Criticism,* ed. Gayle Greene and Coppelia Kahn (New York: Routledge, 1985), 59–79.

26. Abdul R. JanMohamed and David Lloyd, "Minority Discourse – What Is to Be Done?" *Cultural Critique* 7 (Fall 1987): 10.

27. "Heteroglossia" is Bakhtin's term for the diversity of languages. More specifically, it is the confusion of contradictions that creates the noisy context of any given utterance. These conditions preclude the possibility that any utterance is ever really repeated since the precise matrix of forces can never be entirely recuperated. See Bakhtin, "Discourse in the Novel," 428, and Tzvetan Todorov, *Mikhail Bakhtin: The Dialogical Principle* (Minneapolis: University of Minnesota Press, 1984), 56, 72–3.

28. I am borrowing the terms "authoritative discourse" and "internally persuasive discourse" from Bakhtin, who makes the point that this stratification occurs within each individual. He argues further that

"the importance of struggling with another's discourse, its influence in the history of an individual's coming to ideological consciousness, is enormous." Whereas Bakhtin establishes a binary opposition between authoritative discourse ("the word of the father") and internally persuasive discourse, I add a third – the "silent" word of the mother – to account for her repressed voice in Milkman's growth into consciousness. Moreover, my black feminist appropriation of Bakhtinian theory attempts to correct its blind spot to female voice and to propose an intersubjective alternative to his militaristic oppositional discourse.

29. It is almost impossible to discuss the cultural, social, and political implications of language without an awareness of how feminist criticism has permanently altered how we think and write about language. I have drawn on the work of such theorists as Jane Gallop, Helene Cixous, Julia Kristeva, Jacques Lacan, and others. See Jane Gallop, *Daughter's Seduction: Feminism and Psychoanalysis* (Ithaca: Cornell University Press, 1982), 47. For an excellent review of feminist perspectives on language, see Furman, "Politics of Language," 59–79.

30. Bauer, *Feminist Dialogics*, xii.

31. Jacques Lacan, *Ecrits*, trans. Alan Sheridan (New York: Norton, 1977), 2. Also see Kaja Silverman, *The Subject of Semiotics* (New York: Oxford University Press, 1983), 126–78, for a detailed discussion of the construction of the self as a subject.

32. See Jessica Benjamin, *The Bonds of Love: Psychoanalysis, Feminism, and the Problem of Domination* (New York: Pantheon, 1988), 30. Bakhtin expresses intersubjectivity through mutual reflection, perception, and aurality. See Todorov, *Mikhail Bakhtin*, 94–8.

33. See Gates, *Signifying Monkey*, 52–3. Also see Geneva Smitherman, *Talkin' and Testifyin': The Language of Black America* (Boston: Houghton Mifflin Co., 1977), 118–34. Although the signifying voice occasionally appears in the third-person voice of the narrator, my focus here, for purposes of explication, is on the actual speech, the spoken discourse, of the characters in the novel.

34. For more on the murder of Emmett Till as a catalyst for the Civil Rights Movement of the late fifties, see Henry Hampton and Steve Fayer, eds., *Voices of Freedom: An Oral History of the Civil Rights Movement from the 1950s through the 1980s* (New York: Bantam Books, 1990), 1–15.

35. See Richard Wright, *Native Son* (New York: Harper and Row, 1940).

36. Smitherman, *Talkin' and Testifyin'*, 104.

37. For a useful discussion of how gender and domination operate in

culture to create false dichotomies such as self and other, private and public, autonomy and attachment, see Benjamin, *Bonds of Love*, 204.

38. Kaja Silverman, *The Acoustic Mirror: The Female Voice in Psychoanalysis and Cinema* (Bloomington: Indiana University Press, 1988), 100.

39. The term "griot" is familiar to most scholars of African American literature as the "oral historian and educator in African society." For a definition and discussion of this figure, see *Talk That Talk: An Anthology of African-American Storytelling*, ed. Linda Goss and Marian E. Barnes (New York: Touchstone, 1989), 179–81.

40. See Bauer, *Feminist Dialogics*, xiii.

41. For an excellent dialogic reading of *Sula* and a useful discussion of the implications of reader-response theory for reading African American literary texts, see Deborah E. McDowell, "Boundaries: Or Distant Relations and Close Kin," in *Afro-American Literary Study in the 1990s*, ed. Houston A. Baker Jr. and Patricia Redmond (Chicago: University of Chicago Press, 1989), 51–70.

42. Morrison, "Rootedness," 341.

43. See Bakhtin, *Speech Genres and Other Late Essays*, 94.

44. Henderson, "Speaking in Tongues," 36.

45. Clifford, *Writing Culture*, 12.

4

Knowing Their Names:
Toni Morrison's *Song of Solomon*

MARIANNE HIRSCH

That is the ability we must be on guard against for the future – the female who reproduces the female who reproduces the female.
– Toni Morrison

Wherever human society wishes to move into an articulation, the Father must discover and humbly observe his limit.
– Hortense Spillers

Why they got two words for it 'stead of one, if they ain't no difference?
– Toni Morrison

The "absence" of fathers permeates feminist stories.
– Sara Ruddick

1
Daddy

IN the introduction to her collection of black feminist theoretical essays, *Changing Our Own Words*, Cheryl Wall identifies 1970 as a moment of origin for "a community of black women writing."[1] Novels, autobiographical texts, essays, and poems which appeared during that year shared thematic focal points: "the exploration of family violence, sexual oppression and abuse, and the corrosive effects of racism and poverty." What is more, they envisioned black female characters as survivors – active agents in the struggle for social change. In exploring the texture of familial interactions and in placing women in positions of centrality, however, these texts formed a community which appeared deeply threatening to male readers. As Deborah McDowell argues in the same collection, women's writings that concentrate on the domestic space of home also reveal that space as "the privileged site of women's exploitation."² McDowell traces black male critics' responses to these texts, exposing their obsessive desire for the recuperation of the patriarchal family, for the restitution of the father's dominant place. African American women's experiences within the construct of family have been buried, she insists, and only now, since 1970, have women's subordination and victimization within the familial plot begun to emerge into view, thereby frustrating the desires of male readers for unequivocally positive images.

Toni Morrison's novels systematically interrogate a range of familial roles and representations: her project, it would seem, is to define African American family romances in the aftermath of slavery and in the context of twentieth-century economic and social pressures, shaped by racism and sexism. Morrison's narratives penetrate to the subconscious aspects of familial interaction, even as they place family firmly within the space of community and society. Her novels juxtapose the realities of African American family relations to hegemonic family romances, to the dominant mythos of the patriarchal nuclear family which in the ruling culture constitutes the measure of success. In each of her novels, Morrison interrogates that mythos from the vantage point of a socially marginal and economically disadvantaged culture, one whose history radically challenges the very bases on which the mythos of the patriarchal Oedipal family rests. Drawing on multiple mythologies, Morrison's novels refine and redefine the understandings of familial ideology that have dominated during the last thirty years in U.S. culture. Writing of the African American family of the 1970s and 1980s, however, means confronting not only the legacy of slavery and the distortions it performed on all intimate relationships but also the great social and economic pressure in the wake of Lyndon Johnson's "Great Society." It means confronting the stigma of the popularly acclaimed Moynihan report (1965) that labeled the black family a pathological "matriarchy" and failed to claim any public responsibility for the realities: massive unemployment and low pay for African American men and women, poor educational opportunities for black youth, the drug culture, and the resulting pressures placed on familial structures.[3] Instead, Moynihan maintained, and others echoed, the black family's "deterioration" could be explained by rampant sexual debauchery among the black population, by the instability and violence of black men, and by the pathological dominance of black women. McDowell identifies the report as singly responsible for the silences about women's experiences within the family. To write the story of the African American family in the wake of the report and the public images it fostered is always to write against the risk either of perpetuating or of appearing to repress this noxious stereotyping.

In recent years, cultural critics have begun to reveal the racist assumptions that underlie the Moynihan report and subsequent analyses of "the black family," as well as the divergent and incompatible ideologies of family that continue to pertain in the United States. Speaking in particular of the father's complicated role and of father–daughter incest, Hortense Spillers bluntly articulates the methodological difficulties confronting the writer and the critic: "We situate ourselves, then, at the center of a mess altogether convoluted in its crosshatch of historic purposes. There is no simple way to state the case, but crudely put, we might ask: to what extent do the texts of a psychoanalytic ahistoricism, out of which the report, the transaction of incest arise, abrade, reveal against the historic scene and its subsequent drama? Does the Freudian text translate in short (and here we would include the Freudian progeny Lévi-Strauss and Lacan among them)?"[4] The notion of "translation" can only begin to describe the methodological quandary, for the very terms "family," "father," and "mother" signify differently in an African American context than they do in a Eurocentric one. The laws of captivity recognized neither maternity nor paternity, Spillers elaborates, but they made the status of paternity particularly distant from the patriarchal domain reigning in the dominant culture: the mostly illiterate African slave father, dispossessed of his culture and subordinate to the "captor father's mocking presence," transmits neither patronym, logos, nor law to his progeny.[5] Paternity is more than, other than, a "fiction"; it is, in Spillers's terms, a "puzzle." What terms, one

71

might ask, are available to the feminist writer and critic who wishes to discuss this "puzzle" in the 1970s, 1980s, and 1990s?

In *The Bluest Eye*, her first novel, published in 1970, Morrison begins her familial interrogations with one of the most deeply suppressed and unsayable issues in familial representation, father–daughter rape and incest, but here she is clearly more interested in the daughter's story than in the father's. Although her portrayal of Cholly Breedlove is remarkably gentle and even sympathetic, Morrison focuses less on him than on Pecola herself, on *her* dreams, desires, and disappointments. Cholly's devastating role is to act out more directly the humiliation that society has already inflicted on Pecola.[6] In her next novel, *Sula* (1973), Morrison concentrates even more single-mindedly on women. From the self-estranged Shadrack, to the abandoning Boy Boy, Jude, and Ajax, the absent Mr. Wright, the incapacitated Plum, the futureless Chicken Little, to the interchangeable Deweys, Morrison seems systematically to inscribe the incapacity of African American masculinity, even as she writes men out of positions of importance in familial units and women's lives. This is truly a world without fathers. Eva's three-woman family becomes a model which Morrison will repeat in two subsequent novels, a female-headed household that manages without men. Although she is fascinated by this arrangement, Morrison in no way idealizes it. When her central character Sula rejects femininity as defined by heterosexuality, when she dreams of a life outside maternal identification, the novel sympathizes with her but clarifies that this rejection is not, in that context at least, either a viable or a successful choice.[7]

By 1977, with the publication of *Song of Solomon*, however, Morrison radically shifts the focus of her familial portraits to men. More is at stake than the choice of Milkman as the male protagonist of her bildungsroman: it is fathers more than sons who come most clearly into focus. The book's dedication, simply "Daddy," begins to indicate the import and the implications of this new interest. "Daddy," a child's term of endearment, invokes a father who is seen from the perspective of the child, not an authoritative paternal or patriarchal figure. The diminutive "daddy" is the father made small, made to the size of the child, the father who is nurturing and vulnerable at the same time. Nevertheless, the echo of

Sylvia Plath's "Daddy" reminds us of the father's other side, of his authority, his distance, his brutality. In Morrison's dedication, "Daddy," on its own, without the "for" or "to" that is the customary mark of a dedication, amounts more to an address and an appeal, rather than a gift or presentation. This is a novel that explores the formation of masculinity, in relation to the process and the legacy of paternity. And this is an exploration that is addressed to the father. In no way, however, has Morrison abandoned the thematics of female familial life.[8] The space between fathers and children, children and fathers, is still inhabited by women, by mothers, daughters, and sisters: not only by the magnetic Pilate and her three-woman household but also by Ruth Foster and her two daughters. Paternal relations are embedded in a range of other familial interactions, interactions that are dominated by the problems and the prospects of paternity and that both shape and reflect the dimensions of the paternal. The novel's project is to work through this dominance of the paternal and to confront paternal affiliations with other relational paradigms, so as to discover a balance between the extremes of familial interaction, between intimacy and absence, closeness and distance. Its project is to embody the father, to explore the paternal–filial relationship in its bodily manifestation. Its project is to consider the paternal connection to and divorce from the logos and to do so in the context of the politics of literacy.

Song of Solomon radically rethinks familial relations and the process of familial transmission. It participates in what Spillers has called the "romance of African-American fiction[, which] is a tale of origins that brings together once again children lost or stolen or estranged from their mothers."[9] Yet this novel adds fathers to mothers and explores the viability of a dual masculine–feminine legacy. Thus, it at once envisions an ideal of heterosexual understanding and co-implication and painfully and painstakingly demonstrates the difficulties of reaching that ideal within the circumstances of African American life in the 1960s.

"The fathers may soar / And the children may know their names" – the novel's epigraph raises the novel's central themes: family relations, flight, transmission, origin, knowledge, naming, transcendence, contingency. In its two parts, the epigraph confirms the intersections and interconnections between the structures of the familial (paternity, childhood) and the structures of language and the symbolic (naming and knowing). Even as it highlights paternity, however, the epigraph places it at a distance; controversially it condones and supports this distancing: "The fathers may soar." Morrison disturbingly explains this in an interview: "I guess I'm not supposed to say that. But the fact that they [men] would split in a minute just delights me. . . .[T]hat has always been to me one of the most attractive features about black male life." Morrison continues: "One of the major differences between black men's work and black women's work is that the big scene for black men is the traveling Ulysses scene. They are moving. . . . That going from town to town or place to place or looking out and over and beyond and changing – that's what they do."[10] Masculine flight, literalizing an important theme in the African American literary and cultural tradition, dominates the text's beginning, middle, and end. But in this text, flight is both escape and evasion, both transcendence and avoidance. I propose, in what follows, to read the novel through the two parts of the epigraph and to explore, in particular, the novel's models of paternity, its complicated negotiations of paternal presence and absence, and the impact of the paternal on other familial relationships.

My own position as a Euro-American feminist critic of this African American text, my upbringing in a patriarchal nuclear family, and my present situation in a "blended" middle-class family should not be disguised. If indeed, as Hortense Spillers suggests, "the African-American text run(s) parallel to that of a Eurocentric psycho-mythology,"[11] if indeed the history of the African-American family obliges the critic to scrutinize the very terms she uses to discuss its representations, these factors certainly determine my perspective as a "parallel" one: one that runs next to but that does not unproblematically intersect with that of the text. My engagement with the text, therefore, has to be an act of displacement and an exercise in "translation," an exercise in perceiving the simultaneity of likeness and difference. The present context in which we read Morrison's 1977 text, however – the recent resurgence in public scrutiny of the "black family" and its "problems," of which the most pervasively discussed certainly are the father's "absence," the "parallel" crisis in the Euro-American family, and the antifeminist backlash they have caused – makes an engagement with this novel crucial.[12] *Song of Solomon*, I believe, offers ways in which to read aspects of paternity which have heretofore remained untheorized. In allowing us to explore the myths and realities of paternal "absence," this novel retains its topical significance for male and female, black and white readers alike.

2
"The fathers may soar"

"The Macon Deads exemplify the patriarchal nuclear family that has traditionally been a stable and critical feature of Western civilization. The misery of their daily lives demonstrates how few guarantees that domestic configuration actually carries."[13] Valerie Smith's characterization of the Dead family aptly suggests how, in fact, the nuclear patriarchal structure itself creates the problems it is supposed to resolve. Among the many family portraits in the space of the text, the Deads represent, in fact, the only nuclear arrangement. What "deadens" the Deads, however, is Macon, the father: his single-minded ambition, his unscrupulous greed, his unabashed materialism, his lack of nurturance. Macon is the only father in this novel who is present, home with his family; he is the only father who has neither flown away nor been killed nor killed himself. Yet, ironically, his presence is so overpowering as to disable the other members of his family.[14] The novel's images of paternity vacillate between this crushing presence and a devastating absence, between incestuous closeness and injurious distance.

Macon himself admits that he can speak to his son "only if his words held some command or criticism. 'Hello, Daddy.' 'Hello, son, tuck your shirt in.' 'I found a dead bird, Daddy.' 'Don't bring that mess in the house'" (29).[15] Macon's relations with his wife and daughters are so unloving as to have made the latter "boiled dry from years of yearning" (28) and the former "dying of lovelessness" (152). But Macon has been concentrating on another aspect of paternity, the one he wants at all costs to pass along to his son as "what's real": the acquisition of property. "Let me tell you right now the one important thing you'll ever need to know: Own things. And let the things you own own other things. Then you'll own yourself and other people too. Starting Monday, I'm going to teach you how" (55). Macon's slippage between owning "things" and owning oneself and other "people" is remarkable, especially for a descendant of slaves. Yet he believes, wrongly, that he inherited his material ambitions from his own father, Macon Dead Sr., the American Adam who out of nothing fashioned the beautiful farm Lincoln's Heaven, who grew "real peaches," and who was killed because his land was in the white farmers' way. Whereas Macon Sr. owned things that "grew" other things, Macon II aspires to own things that "own" other things and people too.

Macon II's misapprehension, a misreading that clearly echoes the distortions of master–slave relations, is crucial, for his distance from the land and from his past, as well as his obsessive search for urban respectability and success, has changed him, unrecognizably, from a "nice boy," to a "stern, greedy and unloving" man. "Be nice if you could have known him then," Pilate says to Milkman about his father's boyhood. "He would have been a real good friend to you, like he was to me" (39). Throughout the novel, Macon II's paternity is contrasted to that of his own deceased father, Macon Sr., as well as to his own loving fraternal/paternal relation with the young Pilate. "For a dozen years she had been like his own child" (27). "Hadn't been for your daddy, I wouldn't be here today" (40). Macon used to carry the motherless Pilate in his arms to a neighboring farm and then come back to "work right alongside" his father. What that phrase means about father–son connection, Milkman understands only much later when he hears it from his father's childhood friends: "Milkman thought then that his father was boasting of his manliness as a child. Now he knew he had been saying something else. That he loved his father; had an intimate relationship with him; that his father loved him, trusted him, and found him worthy of working 'right alongside' him" (236). Macon Sr. is the father who cooked wild turkey better than anyone, who named his farm Lincoln's Heaven, who warmed his orchard with a fire when the spring was too cold, who trained dogs and horses, who sang like an angel as he plowed forty acres. He is the father who could claim the land and make it his. He is also the father who remained in perpetual posthumous contact with Pilate, guiding her through difficult times with wisdom and intimate care. Unlike his own father, Solomon, Macon Sr. does not fly off and leave his family; he sticks by them in daily and close nurturing protection and care. And his protection is neither too close nor too distant: he knows how to "work right alongside" his son without smothering him or leaving him, offering for the novel a paradigm of successful paternal–filial relation. But it is precisely Macon Sr.'s distinctive relation to property which gets him killed. Since he can neither read nor write, since he does not possess the literacy that will legitimate the power of the logos as he has defined it, he cannot truly own the land he nurtures and cares for. Even while he aspired to success in the terms of the dominant culture, that is, ownership and material possession, he wished to inscribe that success with his own mark of difference: he chose nature over the symbolic; he chose to nurture his property rather than to claim it in the terms of the white patriarch's law. The only way the white patriarch can dispossess him of his property, then, is to kill him.

Macon Sr., or Jake as he was called as a child, is himself the victim of paternal abandonment. As a descendant of the fabled ancestor Solomon, father of twenty children, Jake was the last, referred to mysteriously as the "only son": he was the one chosen by his father to accompany him on his triumphant flight back to Africa but was carelessly dropped back in the home the father abandoned. Ever concerned about abandonment ("You can't just go off and leave a body," he keeps repeating to Pilate), he builds a stable, beautiful, and fertile home even without the help of his wife. Nevertheless, he does not succeed in keeping it and in surviving. His history of vulnerability and longing, of warmth and care, his unique relation to property, contributes to the picture of ideal paternity offered by Macon/Jake.

Solomon's own paternity receives contradictory interpretations in the space of the text. His flight, a heroic return to Africa, offers his descendants a mythic form of transcendence with which to identify, an admirable and legendary rejection of his slave condition, a revolutionary rebellion. But his flight can also be seen as an act of paternal irresponsibility and abandonment, especially as it echoes the mock-heroic flight of the insurance agent Robert Smith, with which the novel begins: "But anyway, hot stuff or not, he

[Solomon] disappeared and left everybody. Wife, everybody, including some twenty-one children. . . . It like to killed the woman, the wife. . . . [S]he's supposed to have screamed out loud for days" (326, 327). As Susan Byrd concludes her narrative about Solomon's mysterious flight, she wonders about Ryna's screams: was she the kind of woman who could not live without a particular man, or was she distraught by having to take care of twenty-one children by herself? In allowing Susan to pose this question, the novel qualifies the option of flight even as it features it – in the novel's epigraph, its beginning, and its end. Heroic soaring is also antiheroic evasion.

These contradictory paternal images come together in another figure we encounter only in various narratives and legends throughout the novel: the town's first black doctor, Dr. Foster. Foster nurtures not only his only daughter, Ruth, but also the rest of the black population, for he cares for the sick and delivers all the babies. Yet, arrogant and disdainful of his patients, he "flies off" in his own way through his self-destructive and escapist dependence on drugs. Even with Ruth he is unable to find an acceptable delimitation between paternal love and transgressive incestuous closeness. As he welcomes Macon Dead's attentions to his daughter, he thinks less of her than of his own disturbing confusion:

> Her steady beam of love was unsettling, and she had never dropped those expressions of affection that had been so lovable in her childhood. The good-night kiss was itself a masterpiece of slow-wittedness on her part and discomfort on his. At sixteen, she still insisted on having him come to her at night, sit on her bed, exchange a few pleasantries, and plant a kiss on her lips. Perhaps it was the loud silence of his dead wife, perhaps it was Ruth's disturbing resemblance to her mother. More probably it was the ecstasy that always seemed to be shining in Ruth's face when he bent to kiss her – an ecstasy he felt inappropriate to the occasion. (23)

Is it appropriate for Doctor Foster to be delivering his own granddaughters, to be there when his daughter "had her legs wide open" (71)? Was Ruth naked in bed with her dead father when Macon walked in, as he claimed, or was she, as she insists to her son, kneeling in her slip sucking his beautiful fingers, the only part of his body not puffy from ether? As it fails to settle these questions, the novel acts out the confusion between closeness and distance that it tries in different ways to resolve. When she goes off to lie on her father's grave at night, as though to meet a secret lover, Ruth insists that he was the "only person who ever really cared whether I lived or died. . . . When he left [this world], I kept on reigniting that cared-for feeling that I got from him" (124). Here, Ruth expresses a daughterly yearning that dominates the novel's filial emotions, the need for continued and close paternal bodily closeness.16

The incestuous confusion of distance between Ruth and her father is perpetuated in her relationship with her son and is responsible for his name, "Milkman." It is here that the confusions between closeness and absence which define paternal relations extend to and shape a number of other familial interactions. Ruth's secret and transgressive nursing feels to Ruth not only like "a balm, a gentle touch," but also like an act of magic and creativity. As Ruth's imagination equates nursing with spinning gold, she places herself in a heroic tradition of fairy tales which the novel juxtaposes to the masculine heroism of flight. In "Rumpel-stiltskin," spinning gold successfully is the miller's daughter's way of staying alive. In outwitting the spirit who helps her and in "knowing his name," she manages to keep her child and to care for him. This is the tradition of domestic heroism with which Ruth identifies but which the public world delegitimates when Freddy voyeuristically and mockingly intrudes on the mother and growing son. Some appropriate but undefinable balance of closeness and distance is violated during those moments of nursing, a balance no relationship in the novel except the two Macons' brief and endangered "working alongside" can successfully reach.

If parent–child relations are subject to the risks of incestuous familiarity, brother–sister bonds are equally endangered in this complicated father-dominated familial landscape. Milkman comically performs an act of fraternal transgression when he urinates on his sister Lena and kills her plant, symbolically making her sterile. Milkman's love for Hagar is doomed because they are too closely related: " 'This here's your brother, Milkman.' . . . 'That ain't her brother, Mama. They cousins.' The older woman spoke. 'Same thing.' . . . 'Then why they got two words for it 'stead of one, if they ain't no difference?'" (43, 44). When Hagar's love starts getting boring and flat, it is because it is too familiar, because she has stopped introducing distance by refusing. Pilate's questions to Hagar celebrating their similarity could equally well elicit the opposite of the answers she intends: "'How can he not love your hair? It's the same hair that grows out of his own armpits. The same hair that crawls up out of his crotch on up his stomach. . . . It's his hair too. He got to love it'" (319). This sameness, beautiful to Pilate and to Hagar, but unwanted by Milkman, can only be broken by extreme familial violence, a violence expressed first in Milkman's cold and formal letter of disengagement, then in Hagar's ritualized and unrealized murder attempts, and ultimately in Milkman's shocking suggestion to her that she insert the knife in her own crotch. Indirectly, of course, she does just that when she kills herself after first attempting to make herself into an object of desire, introducing the objectifying distance of clothes, makeup, and media images between herself and her incestuous lover.

The transgressive and uncomfortable nature of Milkman and Hagar's relationship mirrors the marriage of their ancestors Macon Sr. and Sing and explains perhaps the mystery of their legendary history. If Macon/Jake and Sing grew up together in Shalimar, why did they tell everyone in Pennsylvania that they met on the wagon of ex-slaves going north? And if Macon/Jake was born in Shalimar, why did he say he was from Macon? And why was Sing so insistent that he keep his lugubrious attributed name Macon Dead; why was she so eager for a new start and a clean slate? Although Milkman raises these questions, his quest yields no satisfactory answers. His quest implies, however, that their quasi-incestuous upbringing could be the key, that if they were to establish what may have felt like an incestuous marital bond, it had to be in secrecy and in a new place.

The great preponderance of incestuous connections in the novel, from the ancestors to the youngest generation, constitute one side of familial configuration; escape, distance, and death constitute the other. That "inexorable play of sameness, of identities misplaced and exchanged," that is incest is inadequate as a figure on which to base cultural formation: culture requires articulation and differentiation.[17] But flight is equally problematic, for differentiation must, in turn, be based on connection. Two figures can perhaps serve as objective correlatives, as incarnations, of the contradictory familial images the novel develops: Pilate's smooth stomach and the dead body of Guitar's father. Together they make it possible to think through the gendered nature of relationships, as well as the particular role of the paternal in the vacillation between presence and absence, sameness and difference, which seems to define all intimacy in the text.

When Pilate "birthed herself," she broke her interconnection with the dead mother. Because it is a sign of lack, of an absent connection, her absent navel and the absent cord it implies are utterly threatening to everyone around her. No one can come into the world already cut loose. But Pilate has amply compensated for her lack: her father's and brother's nurturing closeness provided her with the intimate bond she missed. When her father is killed, however, she needs artificially to create a bodily connection to him and perhaps, by extension, to her mother. When she pierces her own flesh with the earring which, shaped like a womb and connected to her body like an umbilical cord, contains her name, she repairs the absence of relation that has failed to mark her body. By placing her name in her ear, moreover, she can literally incorporate the father's word, make it flesh.[18]

The body of Guitar's father – sawed in two by a sawmill, with the two halves no longer fitting together – serves as another paradigmatic image in the novel's analysis of relationships. This one, however, is marked as masculine and as paternal; it demonstrates, moreover, the ways in which the family, by way of the father, is embedded in larger social and economic forces. Guitar is permanently shaped not so much by the loss of his father but by the contradictions of his father's death, by the lack of fit: the candy offered the children by the mill owner in exchange for their father, the money offered their mother and her accepting, grateful smile. What is wrong here, what Guitar literally cannot swallow when he rejects candy, is the father's unnatural death in the service of white capitalist patriarchal production and consumption and the intervention of the white industrialist who equates the black male with cash and candy.

The death of Guitar's father, like the murder of Macon Dead II at the hands of the Butlers, points to the social plot which exists outside, but which is interwoven with, the familial. It is the plot of the dominant culture, which is threatened by African American adult masculinity and entrepreneurial spirit. The play of sameness and difference within the black family, then, is always overshadowed and interrupted by another dominant and controlling term: the white patriarch protecting "his" property. It is when he, or his machine, saws the black man in two or shoots him five feet into the air or lynches him that he reestablishes his single authority. But the black man's parts never fit; his body does not stay buried. And the black man's son or daughter needs to try to make sense of this puzzle. Unlike Pilate, Mr. Bains cannot repair the damage done to him. In the vocabulary of this novel, men, especially men who are fathers, are more deeply implicated than women in the larger structures of money and power that interrupt and determine the familial plot. African American paternity, as Hortense Spillers claims, is always dual, divided.[19] The father's familial affiliations, much more so than the mother's, the daughter's, or the sister's, are always subject to the demands of this second, social plot. Sawed in two, shot five feet into the air, black men cannot bring into balance the external social threat with the internal familial needs and demands for intimacy. Macon II demonstrates that this lack of fit applies to middle-class black men as well as to the poor and disadvantaged, just as Guitar's involvement with the Seven Days, all men, demonstrates a different response to the dualities and divisions that characterize African American masculinity. Whatever "doesn't fit" in the familial interactions Morrison portrays, then, is much exacerbated in the position of the masculine and the paternal.

The white patriarch's external intervention in the life of the black family explains perhaps the alternative, Oedipal narrative that lies at the origin of Pilate and Macon II's story: the incident in the cave. Macon's primal murder of the ghostlike old white and white-haired man guarding his sacks of gold indeed reads very much like a "parallel" story to that of Oedipus, as well as like a story of misplaced revenge. It is thus, perhaps, that in Spillers's terms, the Freudian text can "translate." The day after their father was murdered by the Butlers, the two children spend the night hiding out in a cave. Like Oedipus at the crossroads, Macon lashes out rather incomprehensibly at an old man he accidentally meets there and kills him unthinkingly. This Oedipus kills not his own father but the white patriarch. He murders the authorial father who killed the black father and who owns the gold and has to guard it against the black father and his children. Like Laius, this paternal figure is the primary aggressor and has a primal guilt for which he must atone. If, unlike Oedipus, Macon never gets the benefit of this murder, however, it is because of Pilate's intervention. This leads to Macon's split with Pilate, his resentment and misunderstanding of her, and his continued yearning for the white man's gold, a yearning he passes on to his son. The daughter/sister refuses to perpetuate father/son conflict even if that conflict has been displaced onto the white father. The daughter/sister understands that the two fathers are interchangeable: although her father was killed by whites, she carries what she thinks are a white man's bones as her "inheritance." But bones are indistinguishable: "I've been carrying Papa?" Pilate incredulously asks after years of a misapprehension which carries no consequence. For her, there is but *one* paternity and it is a double and divided one. Even though its parts cannot be re-membered, they must be kept close and carried along.

When Milkman mistakes the bones for gold, he demonstrates the difference between the masculine and feminine relations to the social: Pilate is content to keep her unidentified bones in her own separate alternative social space; Milkman, on the other hand, wants the money that will buy him a way into social success. Whereas she has brought the "white" man into her space, Milkman wants to take his place.

As he goes back to the South to search for Pilate's gold, he finds, instead, the legacy of ancestral knowledge handed down, not through his father, but through Pilate herself. Milkman's quest involves learning not only about masculinity and paternity but also about femininity and maternity. He needs to resolve these slippages between material and spiritual inheritance, between literal and figural, between masculine and feminine. He needs to perform the reconciliation of Pilate and her brother. These very slippages, however, illustrate the novel's interconnection between familial structures and its structures of signification which need to be read back into the family. The play of sameness and difference that defines familial interaction defines also the act of naming and the process of representation.

3
"And the children may know their names"

"Everything bad that ever happened to him happened because he couldn't read. Got his name messed up cause he couldn't read" (53). In the terms of Lacanian psychoanalysis, the father is the logos, the patronym, the name. He marks the child's entry into the symbolic – that system of signification in which the sign is arbitrary, separated from the referent through multiple substitutions and mediations. It is his status in the symbolic that allows the father to break the relation of sameness and mirroring that at least appears to link the child and the mother. Through this necessary break, the father introduces the child into the culture he makes possible. The father, moreover, represents not only the logos but the law. But what of the father who does not read or write, yet who lives in a culture where writing, as Henry Louis Gates Jr. has shown, is the visible sign of reason and of humanity?[20] What of the illiterate father who is excluded from the law except as its victim?

In Morrison's novel, this father, robbed of his authoritative power by his subordinate social status, attempts, on the one hand, to establish his own paternal authority in the terms of the culture which excludes him and, on the other, to challenge that culture by flying away from it. Solomon flies off to Africa, defying the rationality which undergirds every Western belief system. His own name – Solomon, or lawgiver – gets modulated throughout the novel by its sound, becoming Shalimar, Sugarman, Charlemagne. Yet his name raises the question of whether, if he could, he would be the Lacanian lawgiver, of whether he is "saved" by his oppression. His son Jake attempts to assimilate and to become the patriarch: he accepts the arbitrary name given him erroneously by the drunken white officer, a name which results from a misreading of the columns of the bureaucratic form which has become his identity. And he passes that name down to his son, who will transmit it to his son as well. To name his daughter, he steps into the symbolic through the mediation of the Book, the Bible. He wishes to make his act of naming as arbitrary as he knows the hegemonic system of signification to be. Yet, as he does so, some of his own tradition, where words and things are acquired less arbitrarily – his Native American mother's name is Singing Bird; his uncle's name is Crow – intrudes, complicating the process. Macon II remembers how his father

> chose a group of letters that seemed to him strong and handsome; saw in them a large figure that looked like a tree hanging in some princely but protective way over a row of smaller trees. How he had copied the group of letters out on a piece of brown paper; copied, as illiterate people do, every curlicue, arch, and bend in the letters, and presented it to the midwife. (18)

In naming Pilate, Macon Sr. chooses a figure that is as nurturing and protective as he is toward her: the larger tree seems protectively to hover over the smaller ones. Every time Macon Sr. attempts to use the symbolic, however, it tricks him. He goes to Pennsylvania because he cannot read the signs for Boston; he names his daughter Pilate because he cannot recognize the name of the Christ-killer; he signs away his right to his land, because the white neighbors exploit his illiteracy. Yet his son, who can read and manipulate the system for his own benefit, nevertheless perpetuates this paternal tradition of naming his daughters arbitrarily after the first word he points to in the Bible: Magdalene and First Corinthians. Pilate herself still follows, though rather more cautiously, her father's naming practice. She gives her daughter, Rebecca, a biblical name but asks someone for some suggestions and chooses one that sounds good rather than one that looks good or the first one her finger hits.

All of the characters' relations to the unreliable and inhospitable process of symbolic substitution are uncomfortable; each feels a more intimate bond with or a nostalgia for a more literal connection to language and naming.[21] Although she can never claim her own act, Ruth unwittingly renames Milkman through her act of nursing, repossessing him from the symbolic, connecting him to her with a stream of milk, an alternative to the ink the fathers, white and black, use to write their children's names. The community engages in a similar act of repossession when they name their street "Not Doctor Street" or the hospital "No Mercy." In Shalimar, Milkman discovers the power of this literal connection between signifier and referent when he meets Sweet. Pilate also can be "pilot"; she can "sing," thereby literally becoming her mother. The nostalgia for the literal is expressed in numerous acts of metamorphosis which are acts of materialization and literalization: Pilate carries her father's memory in the bag of bones, Milkman keeps Hagar's hair, Ruth sucks her father's fingers and lies on his grave, Pilate carries her name in a box in her ear, feeling its connection as she marks/infects her flesh with it.

Empowered by these close material connections, the characters seem to yearn for more authentic, less distant and arbitrary names and words. The bond with the land Milkman achieves during the hunt leads him to fantasize an alternative system of communication outside the symbolic.

> No, it was not language; it was what there was before language. Before things were written down. Language in the time when men and animals did talk to one another, when a man could sit down with an ape and the two converse; when a tiger and a man could share the same tree, and each understood the other; when men ran *with* wolves, not from or after them. (281)

But analogous to the structure of incest, this literality shares with incest the at once liberatory and deeply problematic challenge to hegemonic cultural structures. As Milkman knows from his own surname, the literal has its own problems; if he rejects the symbolic, then he is already dead, not symbolically deadened by the culture in power, but simply, literally dead. In spite of its pitfalls, the symbolic is, in this novel, the structure that those who are willfully and crucially excluded from it need to confront and come to terms with. But like black paternity, the symbolic in the context of African American culture is also dual and divided: in its fissures, other structures are inscribed and they interrupt and challenge its single and authorial power. Incestuous literality impedes the progress toward culture; distant mediated symbolization deadens and denies vitality and intimacy. *Song of Solomon* searches for the space between, the space of contradiction which can transform and redefine the paternal and, through it, the familial more generally.

How to mediate between the too close incestuous literality of a nonsymbolic nonlanguage and the arbitrariness and uncaring distance that has made the characters "dead" is the project of the novel's quest, the process of "knowing their names." It is a project parallel to and interwoven with the mediation between paternal overpowering presence, on the one hand, and paternal absence, on the other.

> Surely, he thought, he and his sister had some ancestor, some lithe young man with onyx skin and legs as straight as cane stalks, who had a name that was real. A name given to him at birth with love and seriousness. A name that was not a joke, nor a disguise, nor a brand name. But who this lithe young man was, and where his cane-stalk legs carried him from or two, could never be known. (17, 18)

Knowing this young man, this ancestor, is "knowing their names" – a process different from naming or even from renaming.[22] It is a process neither literal as the water stain on Ruth's table, which spreads across the fine wood even as it symbolizes the stain on the family, nor figural as her dead velvet flowers, which have never had an anchor in nature or the real. It is a process that *reads* within the symbolic a connection to a literal which interrupts, disturbs, and challenges its hegemony.

> He read the road signs with interest now, wondering what lay beneath the names. The Algonquins had named the territory he lives in Great Water, *michi gami*. How many dead lives and fading memories were buried in and beneath the names of the places in this country. Under the recorded names were other names, just as "Macon Dead," recorded for all time in some dusty file, hid from view the real names of people, places, and things. Names that had meaning. No wonder Pilate put hers in her ear. When you know your name, you should hang on to it, for unless it is noted down and remembered, it will die when you do. (333)

Milkman reads throughout his journey; he reads road signs, the song, the name of the father and the mother. As Milkman reads, as he discovers the meanings and the names beneath, he engages in the process of "knowing their names" as this novel defines it. Through a complicated process of reading, this process modulates literal and symbolic. It does not totally give up literal connection but insists on undertaking the long, exhausting, and necessary journey through symbolic substitution; it reaches Lacanian language by way of slavery's heritage of illiteracy, thus making that heritage useful and powerful rather than disempowering.

"Knowing their names" is a reading process full of dangers and pitfalls, full of misreadings and wrong turns. It is never complete. The arbitrary play of substitutions that is the symbolic and the literal connections of sameness each threaten to explode into violence. How are we to read the numbers game played by the Seven Days? In the absence of legal recourse, they insist on avenging black deaths on the same day and within the same category, little girls for little girls; but that system of literal substitution bypasses any notion of guilt or innocence, and the people who actually die are not the ones who committed the murders; they are their substitutes. And how are we to read Guitar's final fraternal attack on Milkman? Milkman did not in fact cheat the Days; there was no gold. Yet Guitar still insists that he needs to kill him. First, he erroneously and arbitrarily, symbolically, kills Pilate. If he then needs Milkman's life, is it to create a space of distance between them, separating himself from their fraternal closeness? Or is it to kill off that part of himself which is Milkman and the skeptic about the Days' project? Is Milkman's intended death as arbitrary and symbolic as the other Days' executions, or is it literally a punishment? Does he, in fact, die, or does he fly, bridging the valley that separates him from his alter ego? The novel does not determine this end for us but remains inconclusive, undecidable, unreadable. Yet it ends in several moments of nurturing and connection, between Milkman and Pilate, between Milkman and Guitar, and between Milkman and Solomon/Shalimar/Sugarman/Charlemagne. Milkman's final leap is not a flight away from home; it is a flight toward his past and toward Guitar. It is a leap into a landscape that responds by literally *saying* "tar, tar, tar," that echoes the cries not for death but for being "am, am, am am," and "life, life, life, life."

Milkman's quest is the child's quest for his name and for his father's name. It is a journey of substitutions: knowledge for gold for all his possessions, Shalimar for Danville, cars for buses for planes, legs for cars, and so on. As a journey, it is also an act of reading, of understanding the song he has always known, a song the children used to keep their father's story of leaving alive. It is a journey back over his own life, to understand his own misunderstandings, especially his devaluation of the women who nurtured him; Pilate, his mother, Hagar, his sisters. His search leads him back to Jake and Sing, to his father and to Pilate, to these brother–sister pairs who were so dangerously close as to have been violently separated by death or quarrel. Is his ancestor Shalimar or Solomon or Charlemagne or Sugarman? Whose legacy does he fulfill when he flies at the end, Solomon's or Singing Bird's? These slippages remain important because they define the difficulties of articulation Milkman cannot resolve. What they mark is the fantasy, and in some sense the realization, of a dual inheritance, masculine and feminine, a different duality which supports, supplements, and multiplies the fractured and ultimately debilitating duality of the paternal.

More than Milkman, the novel's end features Pilate, her loving connection to humanity and her death. Burying her father's bones allows Pilate herself to die. Before she does so, she tries to bury her name and earring, no longer needing its material connection to the past and to the paternal naming practice. But a bird (her mother?) comes to reclaim the earring, and the name, from the father's grave, where Pilate had thrown it. As Milkman sees it, he understands that "[w]ithout ever leaving the ground, she could fly" (340). As Pilate becomes her mother, Singing Bird, Milkman can claim this maternal legacy as well, and he does so when he transforms the song and sings it to Pilate: "Sugargirl, don't leave me here." " 'There must be another one like you,' he whispered to her. 'There's got to be at least one more woman like you'" (340), Milkman wishfully asserts. Is the novel suggesting that he himself is, could be, might be, that other, female figure? When Milkman ambiguously and contingently accepts this maternal heritage along with the paternal, the novel re-members the heterosexual bond of transmission that was broken when Sing dies, when Macon leaves Pilate, when he stops making love to Ruth. As it does so, the novel successfully transforms the paternal.[23]

Ironically, however, this heterosexuality does not lead to generation. Milkman, the male protagonist, alone benefits from the lessons learned. Hagar's own quest is only a mock-heroic/tragic version of Milkman's: as she returns from her shopping spree in the rain, she also loses her clothes and possessions, but only to arrive home a ridiculous and suicidal mockery of the sexual object featured by the advertising industry. In spite of their elaborate education, Lena and Corinthians also do not share in the benefits of the knowledge Milkman has been allowed to earn. When Hagar dies, when Lena and Corinthians fail to have children, when Milkman ambiguously leaps and soars, the impossibility of transmission is clarified. The novel has not yet found a way to think beyond the perspective of the child whose invocation, "Daddy," forms its dedication – beginning and end. And although the novel has allowed the male children to know not only their own names but also their mothers' and their fathers', it has not done the same for the female children. It has not yet found a way to share the son's knowledge with the daughter. Although it has deconstructed the dichotomy between the material presence of the mother and the legendary, symbolic absence of the father, it has not yet found a way to incarnate that more embodied yet still comfortably symbolic form of paternity. For that, *Song of Solomon* insists, African American masculinity is still too deeply threatened and endangered.

NOTES

1. Cheryl Wall, "Introduction: Taking Positions and Changing Words," in *Changing Our Own Words: Essays on Criticism, Theory, and Writing by Black Women*, ed. Cheryl Wall (New Brunswick: Rutgers University Press, 1989), 2.
2. Deborah McDowell, "Reading Family Matters," in Wall, ed., *Changing Our Own Words*, 86.
3. Daniel Patrick Moynihan, *The Negro Family: The Case for National Action* (Washington, D.C.: U.S. Government Printing Office, 1965).
4. Hortense J. Spillers, "'The Permanent Obliquity of an In(pha)llibly Straight': In the Time of the Daughters and the Fathers," in Wall, ed., *Changing Our Own Words*, 130, 131. This essay originally appeared in Lynda Boose and Betty Sue Flowers, eds., *Daughters and Fathers* (Baltimore: Johns Hopkins University Press, 1989).
5. Hortense J. Spillers, "Mama's Baby, Papa's Maybe: An American Grammar Book," *Diacritics* vol. 17, no. 2 (Summer 1987): 80.

6. For an interesting analysis of the other father in the novel, Mr. McTeer, and of his own inconsequence, see Vanessa D. Dickerson, "The Naked Father in Toni Morrison's *The Bluest Eye*," in *Refiguring the Father: New Feminist Readings of Patriarchy*, ed. Patricia Yaeger and Beth Kowaleski-Wallace (Carbondale and Edwardsville: Southern Illinois University Press, 1989).

7. See Marianne Hirsch, *The Mother/Daughter Plot: Narrative, Psychoanalysis, Feminism* (Bloomington: Indiana University Press, 1989), esp. Chap. 5.

8. When asked in an interview why she chose a male protagonist for this novel, Morrison responds: "I chose a man to make that journey because I thought he had more to learn than a woman would have." See Nellie Y. McKay, "An Interview with Toni Morrison," *Contemporary Literature* 24, no. 4 (1983): 428.

9. Spillers, "The Permanent Obliquity," 148.

10. Robert Stepto, " 'Intimate Things in Place' – A Conversation with Toni Morrison," *Massachusetts Review* 18 (1977): 487. For a brilliant reading of the novel in relation to the "Ulysses scene," see Kimberly Benston, "Re-weaving the 'Ulysses Scene': Enchantment, Post-Oedipal Identity, and the Buried Text of Blackness in Toni Morrison's *Song of Solomon*," in *Comparative American Identities: Race, Sex and Nationality in the Modern Text*, ed. Hortense J. Spillers (New York: Routledge, 1991).

11. Spillers, "The Permanent Obliquity," 148.

12. See especially the January 25, 1986, CBS Special Report by Bill Moyers, "The Vanishing Black Family – Crisis in Black America." For an excellent summary and analysis of the twenty-five-year history of media representations of the black family, see the July 24/31, 1989, issue of *The Nation, Scapegoating the Black Family: Black Women Speak*, edited by Jewell Handy Gresham and Margaret B. Wilkerson.

13. Valerie Smith, *Self-Discovery and Authority in Afro-American Narrative* (Cambridge: Harvard University Press, 1987), 136, 137.

14. See Sara Ruddick's "Thinking about Fathers," in *Conflicts in Feminism*, ed. Marianne Hirsch and Evelyn Fox Keller (New York: Routledge, 1990), 223: "If an absent father is depressingly disappointing, a present father can be dangerous to mothers and their children."

15. Toni Morrison, *Song of Solomon* (New York: New American Library, 1977). References in parentheses in the text will be to this edition of the novel.

16. Morrison explains how important she believes paternal/masculine nurturance to be for women: "Hagar does not have what Pilate had,

which was a dozen years of a nurturing, good relationship with men. Pilate had a father, and she had a brother, who loved her very much, and she could use the knowledge of that love for her life. Her daughter Reba had less of that, but she has at least a perfunctory adoration or love of men which she does not put to very good use. Hagar has even less because of the absence of any relationships with men in her life. She is weaker" (McKay, "An Interview with Toni Morrison," 419).

17. Spillers, "The Permanent Obliquity," 140.
18. In Kimberly Benston's reading, Pilate's absent navel is "a symptom of post-oedipal freedom from the crisis of origination" ("Re-weaving the 'Ulysses Scene,'" 100), the sign of Pilate's alternative mythology and of her different quest.
19. This is Spillers's argument about masculinity in "Mama's Baby, Papa's Maybe."
20. See Henry Louis Gates Jr., "Writing 'Race' and the Difference It Makes," in *"Race," Writing and Difference, Critical Inquiry* 12 (1985): 1–20.
21. For an extended and excellent discussion of the conflicts and contradictions between figurative and literal modes of signification in women's writing, see Margaret Homans, *Bearing the Word: Language and Female Experience in Nineteenth-Century Women's Writing* (Chicago: University of Chicago Press, 1986). For how these contradictions apply in the writing of race and gender, see her recent unpublished article, "'I Was a White Man': Metaphor and the Body in the Writing of Race."
22. Linda Buck Myers suggests that Milkman in fact himself becomes the lithe young man when, in Shalimar, he suddenly stops limping. See "Perception and Power through Naming: Characters in Search of a Self in the Fiction of Toni Morrison," *Explorations in Ethnic Studies* 7, no. 1 (1984): 39–51.
23. Kimberly Benston offers a similar attempt, in what he calls a "womanist rereading," to inscribe the influence of Pilate and the "scene of female instruction" on this "post-Ellisonian" text of African American modernism. See his "Re-weaving the 'Ulysses Scene.'"

5

The Postmodernist Rag:
Political Identity and the Vernacular
in *Song of Solomon*

WAHNEEMA LUBIANO

S O N G of Solomon (hereafter *Song*) is a postmodernist text.[1] But
its postmodernism is specifically structured by the subversive
dynamics of black American vernacular Signifyin(g) (hereafter just
"signifying") and the relation of that signifying to techniques of
postmodernist indeterminacy, fragmentation, pastiche, and irony.[2]
It explores the political complexities of personal, racial, gender,
and group identification; the language obliquely plays – "signifies" – on the uselessness of essentialist constructions of identity
while it dramatizes the empowering effect of flexible and unstable
constructions of the self.

I evoke postmodernism as background for my reading of *Song*
precisely because the conflicted debates over the definitions and
politics of postmodernism offer an interesting context for considering vernacularity and its relation to history and textual manipula-
tions. And I begin here by raising the issues that motivated my
interest in such a reading of this text. If vernacular signifying, as
various studies and theories argue,[3] constantly creates and re-
creates narratives undermining predictable, normative, prescrip-
tive, or commonsense notions of meaning and reality, what might
be its effect on the ways in which a character is constructed in a
black American fictional text? If the characteristics of signifying are
analogous to the characteristics of postmodernism, and we accept
the possibilities of signifying as political (given the relation between the linguistic "play" of a marginalized group and the dominant group's dialect – standard English),[4] what might that suggest
about postmodernism deployed as literary technique(s) and/or engaged in as critical discourse? What makes *Song* a fascinating pro-
ving ground for these ideas? And finally, how might thinking

about these things illuminate a reading of the novel for students, literary critics, and those interested in political interventions in hegemonic literary discourse?

1

What is at stake for positioning a reading of a black American novel within the discourse of postmodernism?[5] I want to begin by looking briefly at David Harvey's critique of postmodernism's relation to modernism.[6] In his attempt to be fair to the possibilities of postmodernism, Harvey lists the horrors that shattered the optimism of believers in the Enlightenment and modernism, notably Condorcet and Habermas.[7] But his list of *twentieth*-century horrors – "death camps and death squads, its militarism and two world wars, its threat of nuclear annihilation and its experience of Hiroshima and Nagasaki" – passes over the sixteenth through nineteenth centuries' European and Euro-American genocide of the indigenous American population and slavery, both examples of on-the-ground facts of history for two particular marginalized groups in the United States. Those particular histories indicate that at least 350 years ago some of us were already in training to be both cynical about the Enlightenment and less than optimistic about modernism. My awareness of those histories, then, tempers any enthusiasm that I might feel either for harangues against postmodernism that see it as simply recuperating nostalgically the idea of metanarratives[8] or for celebrations of postmodernism that, as Cornel West argues, want to replace modernism with a valorization of "everybody's" (or universal) difference: a naive "we are all marginal" sloganeering.[9]

But to return to Harvey's cautionary notes – he warns that "any postmodern novel focuses on masks without commenting directly on social meanings other than the activity of masking itself."[10] Harvey is simply wrong to state that a focus on masks precludes direct commentary on social meanings – for some groups masking *is* a comment on social meanings. Further, within the terms of black American vernacular, which moves along lines of indirection – or what could be called verbal masking – *commenting directly on something* has often been a luxury denied to black Americans. And direct commentary from the dominant group about black American cultural practices has generally meant that such production has had imposed on it particular conventions which reflect ignorance of or which ignore the historical uses of indirect commentary.

Against Harvey's denigration of postmodernism, I want to consider black American postmodernism not only as a moment when modernism's intellectual and cultural hegemony[11] is at least being questioned but as a general epistemological standpoint for foregrounding what has been left out of larger discourses, a consideration of certain kinds of differences, and the reasons for their absences from those larger discourses. Hal Foster's work on postmodernism articulates the possibilities of postmodernism's resistance, a possible resistance that overlaps with the equally subversive potential of vernacular signifying.[12] The discourse of postmodernism (which is larger and more complex than any simple deployment of postmodernist textual techniques) presents itself as a site for thinking about difference. If postmodernism marks an "incredulity toward metanarratives,"[13] it is also an appropriate description for black American cultural practices whose status in Eurocentric meta- and master narratives has been at best problematic and at worst has been used to justify black American oppression and cultural marginality. Our history shows that we have maintained a fairly consistent level of incredulity toward such narratives; perhaps it is time that the "West" caught up with us. No, the ending, or more to the point, the complicating of modernism's cultural authority is not a crisis for black Americans. The collage modality[14] of postmodernism and the slipperiness of vernacular signifying are ways to refuse the dangerous and simplistic pleasures of authoritative coherence by demanding instead constant restructuring.

As a postmodernist and vernacularly structured text, *Song of Solomon* dramatizes the deconstruction of narrative convention, the complications of race, and the struggles over identification in ways that bring to narrative life the nexus of the personal and the political.

2

That the vernacular exists as a discourse parallel to standard English dialect is important, but equally important is the *manner* in which it exists. Vernacular language moves along lines of alteration, maintaining contradictory, ironic, oblique stances vis-à-vis experience, narration, or even assumptions about reality. By doing so, the vernacular is perfectly constituted to undermine ironically whatever dominant language form it employs. In other words, it stands in deconstructive relation to the dominant language whether by using the dialect and syntactical structure of "black English" or by subverting standard English dialect. In this way, the vernacular reflects the defensive status and indirect stance of its users.

The political implications of vernacular signifying for discussion of race and culture are tremendous. When one signifies in the public domain – with an owner, employer, or within the pages of a text – one is intervening politically as well as artistically. As the basis of a critical apparatus, signifying allows us to debunk the fallacy that it is only the "stuff" of black American lives that is art; signifying is a mode of vernacular artistic production as well as a mechanism for "on-site" metacommentary. Signifying redefines racial differences as cultural difference, with all of the complexities entailed in such a recategorization, and puts our notions of reality up for grabs.

When Guyanese novelist and critic Wilson Harris describes the "commonsense" notion of reality as an "obsessive centrality" which can be subverted by language, "the ground of an interior and active expedition through and beyond what is already known,"[15] he is describing also the deliberately encoding project of the primary mode of black American vernacular – signifying – a dynamic that is subversive in intent and in practice. Signifying deliberately replaces what is being asked, asserted, understood, with something else – as though the utterance itself were only the departure point for an engagement in language that interrupts the fixity of representation to allow for exploration of complexity instead of an acceptance of oversimplified notions of the human self-reality that is identity.

Song complicates the issue of identity-creation by decentering Euro-American systems of oppression within the novel. I do not mean to say that social oppression does not exist in the text; the oppression that racism manifests is part of the content (explicit and implicit) of the novel from the beginning. But I do not think that identity in this novel can be conceived simply in opposition to an oppressive force (with its genesis in the dominant culture) that balks the emergence of a self. The text does set up an expectation of an oppositional construction. It begins with its focus in a black community that is defined narrowly and in negative reaction to a larger community. It is *not* on the right side of the tracks of that community, its main thoroughfare is "Not Doctor Street," and the hospital which is genesis to both the text and the protagonist is "No Mercy Hospital."[16] That oppositional position, however, while conspicuous, is only part of the text's complications. The novel explores the political ground of cultural identity explicitly in terms of vernacular structure, character identity, and political formation. It does so by refusing to allow the reader to ferret out the "truth," the "real" story, the solution to the enigma(s).

The decentering of oppression of which I spoke is parallel in structure to the decentering of the self. Characters must find their ways through the morass of that which defines them just as the black American community outside as well as inside the text must think its way through the various possibilities of political strategies. These two parallels meet in Pilate and Milkman's fates. The text invites a reader to make the first moves toward a reconception of political subjectivity as it examines the fractured and fragmented threads of public and personal history.

It is a critical commonplace to speak of unity, wholeness, and closure in *Song* and to focus on the mythic appropriateness of a search for group and self.[17] Critics who have done so tend to agree that that closure is proven by the transcendence implied by Milkman's leap "into the killing arms of his brother" in the final paragraph of the text.[18] It seems to me, however, that to refer to that act as transcendent reduces the text to a chronicle of a journey to wholeness that is rewarded by transcendence. Such an interpretation does not do justice to the narrative complexities of the novel.

At the very least, the narrative represents a powerfully explicit attack on the ownership psychology and hierarchical ideology characteristic of a patriarchical and capitalist culture. The ostensible focus of the text, after all, is a black American nuclear family patterned on the dominant culture's model; the problematic of the representation of that family is a critique of the American family myth. That this family is complicated only reinforces the critique of that myth.

Macon Dead, the patriarch of this family, defines himself materially. Although he never accepts anyone else's reading of his character, he lets his property tell him who and what he is. He owns several houses, clenches the keys to them in his fist to remind himself who he is, and is haunted at night as he walks by his houses by fears of being "the outsider, the propertyless, landless wanderer" (27). He takes his family for ritualized Sunday drives in his expensive Packard "to satisfy himself that he was indeed a successful man" (31). He tells his son, "Own things. And let the things you own own other things. Then you'll own yourself and other people too" (55). Of course, the supreme irony is that while Macon thinks of himself as someone who owned enough to marry a doctor's daughter (22–23), in fact, his ownership of property had nothing to do with his ability to persuade Ruth's father to accept him as a suitor: the doctor's desperation did the trick (23).

But ownership, in concrete or abstract terms, is what pins Macon and later Milkman so ruthlessly to the ground. Macon Dead tries to assert his self-worth by owning, without ever realizing that *he* is what is owned by his property, his car, and his houses, just as Milkman too is owned by what he means to others. He is owned by his mother and his lover's desires and needs for him, by the need of everyone around him to mark out their worth against him, or by their tendency to assess his worth in terms of who or what they think he owns. The women of Honore, for example, define Hagar as his "honey pot" and, thus, Milkman as the "man with the honey pot." His ownership and subsequent dismissal of his honey pot "made him a star, a celebrity in the Blood Bank" (301). The tendency to assess Milkman in terms of what he owns can be measured by the jealousy, rage, and envy he inspires in the men who watch him down in Danville, Virginia (266).

Such an economic (albeit important) reading, however, does not in and of itself do enough justice to the complexity of the text. The text extends its critique of ownership ideology as a centering mechanism and, further, explores the educative potential of a de-centering stance by its ruthless exploitation of the possibilities of indeterminacy in form and content. Its formal engagement with signifying far more adequately represents the complexity of black American culture, politics, and constructions of identity than any vision of "truth-telling," a vision for which critics of black American literature from the Harlem Renaissance forward have called. The more interesting vision that I think the text sets before the reader is actually a question: how does one create and sustain a resonant political identity while at the same time subscribing to a rigorously decentering notion of the self? I don't think that *Song* answers this question. Nor does it need to in order to raise the issue. But through the intricacies of its structures and characters, the text explores the issues without valorizing self-transcendence or a centered subjectivity. Thus, it rethinks the notion of radicalism at the same time that is examines the critical, political, and literary issues that are part of black American literary history.

At the same time, this text is a multilayered novel whose two protagonists learn to "read" through the layers of history which surround and intersect their lives. Pilate (from the position of physical and philosophical difference) stands as a marker of a decentered and highly effective political identity but one "whose feet never left the ground," whereas Milkman represents the difficulty of coming to terms with the overdeterminations that construct identity for those not marked by physical or philosophical eccentricity. These two protagonists embody in human terms the slipperiness of reality.

I want to focus on two passages in the text which illustrate the way signifying allows the text to slip outside the constraint of normative reality. It is in considering the interstices between what is "real" and what signifying constructs as additional possibilities of the "real" that we can examine the ways in which political identity both is overdetermined and can be subverted.

Such subversion is illustrated in the first sentence of the text, which begins with an omniscient, signifying consciousness that relates, from a distance and without his participation, the history of Mr. Smith and his attempt at flight. Signifying manifests itself in the insertion of figurative language immediately following the less ambiguous and factual language of the beginning: "The North Carolina Mutual Life Insurance agent promised to fly from Mercy to the other side of Lake Superior at three o'clock." The effect of the insertion of the figurative into the mundane is to force the suspension of the reader's too quick identification, or categorization, of the "real" and the "unreal." The text has left the reader to flounder about, raising any number of possible questions: Are we really supposed to believe this man will fly? Does this narrative believe this? Surely the people in this town don't believe it? Why fly from the mercy of the Lord? Why do it at three o'clock? Does this man really think he's going to fly? If he thinks so, is he crazy? Just who believes this stuff? What the hell is going on? The text leaves open the possibilities of taking Mr. Smith seriously or not taking him seriously. But the reader is free to act as the listener in a signifying exchange – to engage in it and to act, as Mitchell-Kernan has explained, as a judge of the successfulness of a particular piece of signifying. In other words, one can register, and nod at, the signifying of "the other side of Lake Superior" and realize that the "other side" of Lake Superior is Canada,[19] the place for which escaping slaves aimed who were dead set on leaving the "mercy" of Euro-America's alleged "civilization" – the rationale for slavery. And as judge, the reader can respond with "uh huh" to the text's playful dignifying of the impossible (flying) and wait for more.

Signifying as a mode of discourse playfully deconstructs the language of the dominant culture even while it interrogates the politics imbued in that language to specific use. The political world first enters the structure of this community obliquely. The passage that describes the origins of "Not Doctor Street" introduces a not-so-benign neglect of that community, but it also engages a signifying struggle over identity and splendidly illustrates the deconstructive potential of signifying. It begins by describing the scenario, which gets more and more detailed with more and more layers of language and history that continually redefine the narrative purpose of the description. The passage moves from language domain (bureaucratic, for example) to language domain (military history, for another example).

This passage signifies at such a dizzying rate that I can only scratch the surface of its possibilities here. It implies indirect and direct subversion on the part of the residents and those people who write to the residents: their naming and unnaming of city streets. The superficially serious tone, standard English, and anonymous omniscient and bureaucratic-sounding narrative voice all signify on the ridiculousness of the entire issue while the passage indicts with indirect contempt official bureaucracies and politicians: "city legislators, whose concern for appropriate names and the maintenance of the city's landmarks was the principal part of their political life, saw to it that 'Doctor Street' was never used in any official capacity" (4). It delineates in detailed fashion the irony of the aid the dominant authorities give to the rebellion by their concretization of resistance to that rebellion: "It was a genuinely clarifying public notice" (4).

Further, the passage signifies on political and historic conditions with its reference to an absence: a time when colored men were not being drafted – which is definitely *not* the time spoken of in the text (1918) – when in fact they *are* being drafted. The language reminds a reader of buried contestation over the rights and responsibilities of "colored" citizens and reminds us of the occasions – World Wars I and II – for that contestation. It signifies on the conception that white city officials have of their black constituency: the notices regarding the official action are posted in "stores, barbershops and restaurants"; they are *not* posted in libraries, schools, or government buildings. History is juxtaposed with present empirical behavior: Mr. Smith climbs onto the roof of a particular hospital at a particular moment carrying his own idiosyncratic history with him. And finally, the reader is caught up in a textual speculation that addresses (at the very least) a different reality: flying.

Flying, however, is not the only focus of textual speculation within the boundaries of the street, its history, or this passage's language. Identity is engaged and reinforced, ironically, by the city legislators, who are not moved to make any material changes in the condition of the lives of this black community – such as desegregating the hospital – but who do try to make their political presence felt by attempting to control the actual physical parameters and boundaries of that community. They do so by attempting to ensure the purity of an identity – a street name; the result of their inept attempts at naming is "read" as vernacular signifying that rhetorically empowers the black community in a way that neither demands a force the community cannot mount nor provokes a backlash from the dominant culture against which the black community might be powerless. Whether the text means us to think that city officials intended to create this parody of municipal intervention or not, the community's critical consumption of and reappropriation of the officials' attempt at narrative alters quotidian reality. It is a naming that unnames as a guerilla tactic.

Rather than mythologizing a black community that does not experience racial oppression, *Song* implies instead the unresolved problems of identity caused by not directly confronting that oppression: the construction of self-, cultural, and political identity while working under the influence of external and internalized oppression. It resists the simplifying tendency of epic mythmaking by anchoring itself within the domestic and restrictive structure of a family romance. It grows from a variation on that structure partially because it is a romance both of an individual and of the idea of choices of political strategies, and partially because whatever consciousness is achieved by the protagonist (and, by allegorical extension, the community) is problematic. The macropolitical world, in fact, is connected to the what, when, why, and who of the text and, by extension, to the personal history of the characters as well as the communal history of the text. Time, history, and the people are all relational, and all through the tapestry are woven the political threads. The text embodies the so easily and often spoken and written truism: the personal is political.

By tying Not Doctor Street and its geographical placement to No Mercy Hospital, the neighborhood's myth of origins as well as its fight for its identity leads literally to the place of the hero's birth and his specific problems of identity. Milkman *is* Not Doctor Street, an allegorical representation of the personal, historical, and political complexities of the construction of identity. This text's structure is finally signifying at its most surgical: it refuses to make itself easily understood.

Signifying language also uncovers subtexts: language withheld from a speech encounter. Guitar attempts to force into the narrative whatever Pilate might feel about his and Milkman's presence in her house by saying, "If you don't want us here, Miss Pilate, we'll go" (37). But Pilate simply replies, "You the one want something" (37), and by *directly* confronting what he had withheld in his statement, his *indirection*, she shifts the ground of the conversation and forces into the open that which had not yet been said by Guitar and Milkman. Guitar was forced to give up on indirection because, as he saw it, Pilate was too direct; but the truth was that Pilate was simply better at being indirect, better at "reading" his indirection. So Guitar "had to pay careful attention to his language" (37).

Signifying works as a potential weapon of protection, with the power to manipulate the way the community perceives a person even when not directly invoked but existing instead as a possible threat in someone's mind: "Macon would put Pilate in jail if he didn't think that she'd loudmouth him and make him seem trashy" (24). Of course, Pilate's loudmouthing language would also speak the "truth": jailing one's sister within the context of this community would be trashy.

The protection of signifying follows one to the grave and protects one from the indignity of being forgotten in one's community. When Hager dies not only does her consciousness leave the text, her funeral seems to indicate that she will be allowed to slip quietly out of existence. It is here that Pilate signifies in the direct sense. She "names" Hagar in this existence in a voice that resonates throughout the church, and throughout the minds of the reader and the participants in the service. She "names" Hagar as a child loved, connected to people, and remembered (318–19), a naming that unnames other community narratives of Hagar.

Signifying language, with its insistent plays on double meanings, also derails important details, causing truths to be withheld. Pilate, the linguistically sophisticated, nonetheless fails to realize for most of her life that although she grieved over not knowing her mother's name, she does, in fact, already know it. She is unaware of her own knowledge because when her father said, "Sing," she assumed he meant the verb and, having missed the "other" possibilities of her father's language, spends most of her life singing and "missing" her mother.

And just as signifying in the vernacular redirects the attention of the speakers and listeners in a constantly shifting fashion so that conversation is ever fluid, and the attention always up for grabs, so too does the consciousness of the narrative itself fluctuate. The text begins, for example, with an omniscient, signifying consciousness that relates, from a distance and without his participation, the history of Mr. Smith and his attempt at flight. Lena and First Corinthians's perception of Macon's car, for example, shifts to Macon's consciousness of it and ends in the consciousness of the people in the community looking at it (31–2).

3

Just as the text shifts consciousness, so too does it blur the lines between political and personal history. Black American history – from the time of the great-grandfather, Shalimar (Solomon), one of the Africans who could fly back home, to Milkman, the man of the 1950s and 1960s – is woven into the text. This span of history provides a political context that serves not only as background but as the medium into and out of which the text fades in its delineation of family, community, and culture. It makes a myriad of political realities an everyday and casual part of the narrative. Lynching is referred to indirectly (as an ordinary fact of life) when Pilate calls Guitar and Milkman the dumbest "unhung" Negroes she'd ever met (37). A political massacre of Irish people is only one of the events that marks the "when" of Pilate's father's death. Another political death and its history, that of Emmett Till, as well as much of the history of black–white social relations, are referred to in street-front discussions among Guitar and other men of the community (80). And Pilate refers to 1963 as the year when she was sixty-eight years old (149), but it is also the year when four little girls were killed in a church bombing in Alabama, so 1963 also marks out the time for Guitar to make his first "kill" as a member of the Seven Days. The political situation of black people in terms of education and employment is indirectly criticized in the representation of the maid's job that First Corinthians has to take because, whether by virtue of having little education or too much education, many black women work as maids.

Politics provides narrative impetus as well as explicit commentary. The Seven Days and capitalist ideology come together because of the need of the Days to obtain capital for a revenge bombing against white people. The political history of black Americans filters into Milkman's history as he learns more of the history of his father's friends when Reverend Cooper talks about his own life while he refers to the violence against black soldiers after World War I (233).

The language of political and economic reality that is prehistory for the boys forms the core of Railroad Tommy's lyrical warning to Guitar and Milkman and is also a site for the change of time. While Railroad Tommy "signifies" on the boys' present petty unfulfilled desires, he scrolls the pages of past history and the reader "reads" Guitar and Milkman's future. He makes visible certain aesthetic pleasures that are part of the workingman's life on the trains in order to make the boys feel the absences of those pleasures, present and future.

Milkman and Guitar, and, by extension, all other young black boys, will not have the pleasure of finished and well-done labor on a railroad as porters in the company of other black men like them because that time has past; they will not have the satisfaction of a return home from that labor; they will not enjoy the comfort and luxury of travel on the beautifully appointed trains (with "red velvet chairs" and "special" toilets and beds) on which black young men like themselves once worked; they will not be the entrepreneurs who can bankroll such travel, such attendants ("a valet, a cook and a secretary"), and such champagne; and regardless of how well and how bravely they serve their country in the military, they will never advance to the status of three- or four-star general. They will not have those things because that is not the way things were for black young men in the 1940s.

History and time in the text move on a number of levels. Although Milkman is the protagonist, and the book ostensibly covers the period of his life, 1931–63, the narrative signifies on his father's life, his grandfather's life, and his great-grandfather's life. Because of the intertwined nature of all of these personal histories, as well as the political context woven into the personal histories, the narrative can be said to cover the history of black Americans. Macon Dead II is the turn-of-the-century New Negro; Jake (renamed Macon Dead) is the slave ancestor who provides the bridge between slavery and Reconstruction; and Solomon (Shalimar,

Sugarman) is the African-born slave who could, and chose to, fly back to Africa.

Time is continually related to macro- and microhistory. The history of Not Doctor Street is tied to the time of Mr. Smith's failure, the birth of the protagonist, the history of the family, and a specific act of racism – the hospital nurse's callous disregard of Mrs. Bains's personal dignity (7).

Time and history are what characters move through as well as back into. Milkman moves forward through the days and weeks of his journey through Virginia to the origins of his family's legends, to a time when history and geography coalesce. In Danville, Virginia, history and time are an overlapping of action, reenacted in modern times by Milkman, and history come to new (his) consciousness.

4

Just as time and political context are both slippery and indirectly revealed in this narrative, so is history. We know, for example, that Milkman is apolitical because he admits it to (and is reproached by) Guitar (101–104), but we also know it because of the relationship of important historical figures to his way of thinking about himself. He romanticizes his slight "deformity" at age fourteen by imagining it as something that he shares with the "late President Roosevelt" (62). But while a fourteen-year-old might be forgiven for preferring romance over political conviction, the person described at the end of this paragraph is an adult – who wears ties, is growing a moustache, smokes cigarettes, and is his father's partner. Time passes, but not the shallowness of Milkman's thinking about his relation to the world.

Despite what Milkman does or does not think about history, despite his boredom with family history – particularly the history of Ruth and Macon's estrangement – he is a participant in not only his own but his community's history. His own birth is a cipher in that history: he was the first black baby born in No Mercy Hospital (9). History, however, is as circumlocuted a part of the text as time. Before Circe is introduced, the reader is told that she gives jam to Pilate. And the narrative defies one to decide what is more important: the history marked by the giving of the jam or the history that Circe embodies? The text not only does not privilege the various components of history but does not facilitate such decision making for a reader.

The blur between historical components – the what happened and the when – is part of the manner in which the text conceptualizes folklore and the interaction of the folk with personal history. And the interaction of folklore with the text is as timeless as the "stuff" of the folk culture. We learn first that Pilate's knowledge of voudou and root magic is responsible for Milkman's conception, and that her use of a voudou doll protects him from further attempts to make Ruth abort the fetus (132); then we read about the root worker who taught Pilate the magic even as she taught Pilate her history (142).

The alliance between folklore and personal history is not allowed to stand as an untroubled one; a concrete manifestation (or lack thereof) of Pilate's personal history – her lack of a navel – and the fear it engenders among the folk cause her to be cast out of that community (143–9). And while Ruth's suckling of Milkman for too long a period of time is a thing "that some of the folk swear by" according to Freddie (14), it is more a manifestation of her need to be touched than an affirmation of folk wisdom.

Although the text asks how one might create a resonant political identity which encompasses one's relation to time, history, and politics, it steers clear of the unhealthy polarities, for example, offered by Macon and Ruth, both of whom are so obsessed with the past that neither can see ahead; Macon, with re-creating the life of his father through land acquisition, and Ruth, with keeping the life of her father before her on the altar of her mind, hold their histories before them and stumble over those histories all through their lives.

If the components of that which we think we know about ourselves and our world – time, history, politics, place, connection, love, and language – are so elastic, the implications for the construction of personal or political identity are staggering, especially when we consider that identity is also fashioned of a person's relationship to what others say or think and what one tries to make of oneself. The text casts identity in terms of what people say about a character, such as what Mrs. Bains says about Macon: "A nigger in business is a terrible, terrible thing to see" (22). Or even what people (signifyingly) say about one's car: "the Packard had no lived life at all. So they called it Macon Dead's hearse" (33). Identity can revolve around what someone names a character, as when Freddie names Ruth's son Milkman (15), or when a drunken Yankee names Jake Macon Dead (18). Or, it can revolve around what someone is able to make of a name: Guitar made "Dead" sound clever (38). Death, on the other hand, can unname someone: "but I don't know her name. After she died, Papa wouldn't let anyone say it" (43). Identity ties a character both to contemporary instrumental function and to larger abstract history. Mr. Smith was both merely "the North Carolina Mutual Life Insurance agent" to everyone in the community *and* the marker for racist insurance practices – because North Carolina Mutual Life Insurance was the first black-owned insurance company. Therefore, Smith, who sells insurance for a black company, also symbolically insures "black life" (3). His inability to fly – in contrast to Solomon's legendary ability to do so – not only opens the text but ties individual anomaly to both economic and folk history.

The most profound relationship between identity and name may be what it is that one makes of one's own name. Pilate, who is connected, responsible, a life-giver and saver, remakes the name Pilate – the Christ-killer, who washed his hands of responsibility. Some characters become what they begin. Guitar, although named for his unfulfilled desire for one, is known to us and to himself as a hunter. He remembers his childhood only in terms of hunting. That was his relationship to the world in the only way we have access to it: his language about what he remembers (85). And one of his few memories of the South is his memory of killing an old doe – a mistake. But a hunter is what he becomes again at the end of the text, a hunter with another kill: another old doe, Pilate, another mistake.

Guitar's identity is as important to this text as Milkman's, because, in this complicated family bildungsroman, their identities, their political selves, represent two polarities. Guitar has a troubled relationship with history. He is uninterested in personal history; his relationship to his past is far less intricate than Milkman's relationship to his own past. He sees his past in the South solely in

108

terms of struggle, and while consciousness of struggle is vital to any political consciousness, the reader has no sense of Guitar's personal involvement within the South. In fact, the only sense we have of Guitar's involvement with anything is his anger. His rage finds its most perfect outlet in the violent struggle of the Seven Days, but he is doomed in the context of the text because of his refusal to "read" various kinds of personal history as potentially or actually political. For him, there is no real difference between the differently political Pilate and the apolitical Milkman.

Guitar devotes his whole life to placing himself (and other black people) in opposition to whites – evening up the numbers –- and so creates for himself an oppositionally defined identity. The Seven Days, in fact, are a logical extension of setting one's life up in opposition to the dominant white culture. In many ways, Guitar's identity is as unified and untroubled by doubt as Macon Dead's is – and ultimately as wrong.

For all his political fervor, however, he is motivated (by the middle of the book) by the most overtly capitalist desires: the gold he thinks Milkman is stealing from him and – according to the way Guitar sees the strategy that he and the other "Days" have put together – from his people. His preoccupation with the "material," with no sense of its corrupting effects on his political practice, complicates any notion of his life as a "pure" political life. And in his reaction to the gold, the implicit similarity of Guitar to Macon Dead becomes explicit. His political practice is not really oppositional, relying as it does on capital accumulation and directed as it sometimes is against members of the same oppressed group for whose liberation he claims to be fighting.

That he can complicate some oppositions, however, is perceivable in the way in which he is able to articulate relationships of place:

> For example, I live in the North now. So the first question come to mind is North of what? Why, north of the South. So North exists because South does. But does that mean North is different from South? No way! South is just south of North. . . . (114)

The irony is that while Guitar can articulate relative and oppositional difference, he cannot "read" the significance of such difference in terms of his own life or the lives of others. What is the difference, finally, between not being white and being black? Meaning does not reside in simple difference; it is how one "reads," what one makes, of the shades of difference. Guitar is involved in overt political action against an oppressor in the crudest possible terms: evening up the sides. In the name of that overt political action, all is sanctioned, even those practices shared by a dominant society that he opposes. So while he hates the oppressiveness of a system that could kill his father and give him candy to sweeten the loss (61), and while he is able to see the inability of the peacock to fly because of all the "shit" weighing it down – a symbol of the oppression of material things – nonetheless, he is ready to kill his brother for the gold that he wants/needs for his political movement. Politics, finally, simply means gold and death to Guitar.

Milkman, the "hero" of the text, is for most of it almost without identity. Milkman begins life in the middle of the battle between Ruth and Macon, and from his entry into the world he *is* their battleground. Further, he is the means of some of his mother's gratification (13) and the reason his lover, Hagar, comes to believe that she was born into this world (136–7). Whereas Guitar constructs an identity for himself that focuses on the political to the exclusion of everything else, Milkman is bored by politics, especially the racial politics that consume Guitar (107). He is uninterested in any but personal history in the most shallow way. He simply wants to remain untroubled by anyone else's stories, anyone else's truth. So his reaction, for example, to the complexities of the conflicting stories of Ruth and Macon is irritation and resentment.

The fact that his attention is so internal and overly pragmatic means that, at the age of thirty, he has to leave home and begin from scratch to construct a self. And in constructing a self he is able to construct an outside world. He is able to see beauty in nature only after it means something to his life. With the hunting and the necessity to prove himself in Virginia, what Kenneth Burke would call another terministic screen[20] moves into place and suddenly the monotony of nature becomes as interesting as the stories to which he becomes privy (273–98). Nature becomes

trees, sounds, man–dog language, and changing light; it is sometimes dangerous but always fascinating, because the land is not
just dirt. It is where one's ancestors farmed, what they loved,
where they died. His learning process begins with learning what
"your people" means (229). And having learned that, he can listen to stories, learn more history, and think outside himself for
the first time in his life.

5

The idea of transcendence implied by flight and so beloved by
many of the novel's critics, and which echoes throughout the story
as a reward, as a hoped-for skill, as an escape, and as proof of
intrinsic worth, is by the end not so clear a proposition. The novel
does end with it but in such a way that the act allows for multiple
and troubling interpretations: suicide; "real" flight and then a
wheeling attack on his "brother"; or "real" flight and then some
kind of encounter with the (possibly) "killing arms of his brother."[21] That Guitar places his rifle on the ground does not make him
any less deadly – his smile and the dropping of the gun both
precede the language of "killing arms" – and his "my man . . . my
main man" is an echo of the same irony that allowed Guitar to call
Milkman his friend even after his prior attempt at killing him
(298).

And Guitar's arms are killing, not just because they want to
answer the challenge posed by Milkman's move toward him, but
because they are the arms that have killed, that killed white
people, that can kill anyone who isn't black, or anyone Guitar can
convince himself isn't black: like Pilate. In other words, Guitar can
make an "other" of anyone who crosses the boundaries of the
definitions he constructs for the group that he purports to love:
black people. What Guitar has constructed in his life is a category
of political ciphers that does not allow for the existence of the
idiosyncratic Pilate or for the existence of the individualistically
apolitical Milkman.

Milkman's journey forward to flight is a journey into his past;
his future is behind him. The text's refutation of the idea of a
whole untroubled self is thus crystallized in the final stop on that

journey. His climactic leap is a move forward which must also be read as a journey back: back to the behavior of a slave ancestor, back to nothingness, back to death.

That this leap occurs over Pilate's body, whose lack of navel has already established her as a myth or a different reality's possibility, further disrupts any optimistically simple reading of Milkman's action as one of untroubled transcendence. Milkman's response to Pilate's death is personal and somewhat selfish. His immediate concern is that there must "be at least one more woman" like her (336). For him, Pilate is subsumed by his desire for what she has meant in his life. So, although he has learned history, in the end Milkman is unable to take that history past the level of personal need. Milkman remains very much the self-concerned individual whose realization of himself as a human collage of history cannot undo his desire to be shown one "true" path to power and understanding.

Pilate, on the other hand, embodies mediating ground between the polarities of Guitar and Milkman and the political selves they represent. She has been, throughout the text, the locus for weaving together history, personal connection, and alternative relationships to time and concrete reality. She lived a political life and represented a funky pastiche of the modern and the folk. Pilate represents, in her knowledge of her world, the ability to manipulate that world, to alter, to make fluid, the real. The results of her ability leave communities and individuals better off than she finds them, more capable of acting in an oppressive set of circumstances.

She remakes the world relentlessly in terms that mean something to her life whether she is equating the blue of the sky to that of her mother's ribbons or dividing the black of night into different shades according to wool or silk she's seen; she allows her life its own reality – and then manipulates it on her own terms. But Pilate dies too. I suggested earlier that the text does not leave us with an answer, a solution, or even a hope.

Song of Solomon resists the pressure to direct our attention to one answer to the questions what is the truth, what is the real story, and how does one act in the face of history? It relentlessly refuses a straightforward answer. It does leave a strong suggestion that flight is not necessarily an untroubled and transcendent response to history regardless of what an ancestor has done. Nor can flight function as an indication of the political possibilities inherent in human interaction with history. The reader learns from Pilate what Milkman heard but did not remember: "You just can't fly on off and leave a body" (147). When successful as escape, flight leaves people behind mourning. When unsuccessful, it leaves people behind dead. It facilitates a final and lethal showdown between barehanded (but not less inimical) friends; however, it is too simple an act to "speak back" to history. It cannot define the extent of one's political being any more than murder can. Finally, it is not around Milkman or Guitar that political possibilities cohere; it is Pilate who, by defying Macon Dead II and intervening in his marriage, is the political agent responsible for Milkman's life. It is Pilate who teaches Milkman to "read" history. And it is Pilate who represents not only embodied history but the praxis that comes with recognizing history's effects, the willingness to theorize about possibilities in the face of history, and the ability to make concrete alternatives to personal and public inequities. Remaining on the ground of history, then, is a labor of love.

NOTES

1. The discussion of postmodernism in this essay is taken from my "Shuckin' off the African-American 'Native Other': What's Po-Mo Got to Do with It?" *Cultural Critique* 18 (Spring 1992): 149–86. I argue there that postmodernism offers a site for African American cultural critics and producers to utilize a discursive space that foregrounds the possibility of rethinking history, political positionality in the cultural domain, the relationship between cultural politics and subjectivity, and the politics of narrative aesthetics.

2. My understanding of vernacular Signifyin(g) is drawn from Henry Louis Gates Jr.'s study *The Signifying Monkey: A Theory of Afro-American Literary Criticism* (New York: Oxford University Press, 1988). Gates is interested in theorizing Signifyin(g) as a dynamic of intertextuality. I am much more interested in using his work to consider intratextual dynamism and the possible politics of Signifyin(g) narrativity.

3. Gates's *The Signifying Monkey;* Claudia Mitchell-Kernan's "Signifying," in *Mother Wit from the Laughing Barrel,* ed. Alan Dundes (Englewood Cliffs, N.J.: Prentice-Hall, 1973); and my own *Messing with*

113

the Machine: Four Afro-American Novels and the Nexus of Vernacular, Historical Constraint, and Narrative Strategy (Ph.D. diss., Stanford University) (Ann Arbor: UMI, 1987) all have that theoretical project in common.

4. See my discussion of black American vernacular in "Henry Louis Gates, Jr. and African-American Literature Discourse," *New England Quarterly* (December 1989): 561–72.

5. The brief discussion of postmodernism in this section is a reduced version of an extended argument that I make in "Shuckin' off the African-American 'Native Other.'"

6. David Harvey, *The Condition of Postmodernity: An Inquiry into the Origins of Cultural Change* (Cambridge: Basil Blackwell, 1989).

7. Ibid., 13.

8. By "metanarrative" I refer to older and well-known narratives that have been the object of discussions and debates for many decades (and, in some cases, centuries); it includes understandings about such preexisting narratives. Some criticisms of postmodernism argue that it is simply a way to restate older mythic stories or histories, understandings about the world, and commonsense ways of seeing the world in newer forms. Metanarratives in this sense are older stories that have their own histories and relationships to certain discourses about them.

9. Anders Stephanson, "Interview with Cornel West," in *Universal Abandon? The Politics of Postmodernism,* ed. Andrew Ross (Minneapolis: University of Minnesota Press, 1988), 273.

10. Harvey, *The Condition of Postmodernity,* 101.

11. I use "hegemony" here as a way to describe modernism's dominance in the cultural explanatory field, a dominance not imposed by a cultural elite but understood and accepted by the majority of art, literary, and cultural commentators/critics as the way to describe the aesthetic and intellectual production of the West over the past century at least.

12. Hal Foster, "Postmodernism: A Preface," in *The Anti-aesthetic: Essays on Postmodern Culture,* ed. Hal Foster (Port Townsend, Wash.: Bay Press, 1983).

13. Jean-François Lyotard, *The Postmodern Condition: A Report on Knowledge,* trans. Geoff Bennington and Brian Massumi (Minneapolis: University of Minnesota Press, 1984), xxiv.

14. "Collage modality" here is meant to indicate the predominance of postmodernism as a style that incorporates the artistic composition of foregrounded fragments as a dominant style and/or aesthetic value in cultural production.

15. Wilson Harris, "Fossil and Psyche," in *Explorations: A Selection of Talks and Articles, 1966–1981*, ed. Hena Naes-Jelinek (Mundelstrup, Denmark: Dangaroo Press, 1981).

16. Toni Morrison, *Song of Solomon* (New York: New American Library, 1977), 4. All further references to the novel will be to this edition and will be cited parenthetically in the text.

17. Such criticism includes Jane Campbell's chapter on *Song* in her *Mythic Black Fiction: The Transformation of History* (Knoxville: University of Tennessee Press, 1986), which argues that the text is an enactment of Milkman's search for identity as "ancestral quest" (136); Barbara Christian's *Black Feminist Criticism* (New York: Pergamon Press, 1985), which refers to the text's resolution of the tension between the "preoccupation with earthly matters and the need to fly" (61); and Joseph T. Skerrett Jr.'s "Recitation to the Griot: Storytelling and Learning in Toni Morrison's *Song of Solomon*," in *Conjuring: Black Women, Fiction, and Literary Tradition*, ed. Marjorie Pryse and Hortense J. Spillers (Bloomington: Indiana University Press, 1985), in which he asserts that Milkman's discovery of "his place in the story of his ancestors" gives him "self-understanding" (193). Dorothy Lee, in *"Song of Solomon:* To Ride the Air," *Black American Literature Forum* 16, no. 2 (Summer 1982), agrees with those and other critics in her reading of the novel as "man's archetypical search for self" in a context of "great myths" that "continue to be relevant to man's questions about his nature and his relationship to self, society, and the universe" (64).

18. See, for example, Lee's *"Song of Solomon:* To Ride the Air," which equates "flight, literal and figurative," with "liberation and transcendence" (70), and Peter Bruck's "Returning to One's Roots: The Motif of Searching and Flying in Toni Morrison's *Song of Solomon*," in *The Afro-American Novel since 1960*, ed. Peter Bruck and Wolfgang Karrer (Amsterdam: B. R. Gruner Publishing Co., 1982), where he refers to "the very notion of flying as a return to one's roots" as that which underlies the action in the novel (299). I could go on, but so much of the criticism repeats variations on these themes that to do so would be pointless.

As a slight variation on the unquestioning acceptance of flight as transcendent good, Grace Hovet and Barbara Lounsberry's "Flying as Symbol and Legend in Toni Morrison's *The Bluest Eye, Sula,* and *Song of Solomon*," *CLA Journal* 27, no. 2 (December 1983), argues that flight as an image of escape or freedom is a "too readily accepted commonplace in Afro-American Studies" (199); however, they too come around to asserting that Morrison moves "toward a more affirmative view of flight . . . which signifies identity, community and creative life" (121).

19. This reading of this line is taken from my 1987 dissertation (*Messing with the Machine*); serendipitously, Morrison herself later articulates the same reading of this line in "Unspeakable Things Unspoken: The Afro-American Presence in American Literature," *Michigan Quarterly Review* 28, no. 1 (Winter 1989): 1–34.

20. Kenneth Burke, *Language as Symbolic Action* (Berkeley: University of California Press, 1966), p. 36.

21. I am not alone in rejecting unproblematic transcendence. Darwin Turner's article "Theme, Characterization, and Style in the Works of Toni Morrison," in *Black Women Writers (1950–1980): A Critical Evaluation*, ed. Mari Evans (New York: Doubleday, Anchor Books, 1984), asks interesting questions about flight.

> What is certain about the scene is that a man like Milkman's father could never ride the air. But will Milkman? Have his new love for his aunt and his reaffirmation of love for Guitar so fortified his soul that he can magically ride the air? Will he discover, in a startled moment as he falls, that his faith could not sustain him? Is he consciously relinquishing his life because he wants to rid himself of the materialism of his mortality? At the beginning of the novel, a Day jumped to his death because he believed that he could fly. Does the ending pessimistically affirm that flight is mere delusion, or does it affirm the theme that one may learn to fly?

Notes on Contributors

Marianne Hirsch is Dartmouth Professor of French and Comparative Literature at Dartmouth College. Most recently, she is the author of *The Mother/Daughter Plot: Narrative, Psychoanalysis, Feminism* (1989) and co-editor of *Conflicts in Feminism* (1990).

Wahneema Lubiano teaches in the Department of English and the Program in Afro-American Studies at Princeton. She is currently finishing a manuscript entitled *Messing with the Machine: Modernism, Postmodernism, and Black American Fiction.*

Joyce Irene Middleton is Assistant Professor of English at the University of Rochester. She is completing a book entitled *The Art of Memory in Toni Morrison's Song of Solomon.*

Marilyn Sanders Mobley is Associate Professor of English and Director of African American Studies at George Mason University. She is the author of *Folk Roots and Mythic Wings in Sarah Orne Jewett and Toni Morrison: The Cultural Function of Narrative* (1991) and several articles on Toni Morrison and other black women writers.

Valerie Smith is Associate Professor of English at the University of California, Los Angeles. The author of *Self-Discovery and Authority in Afro-American Narrative* (1987) and editor of *African American Writers* (1991), she is currently completing a study of black feminist theory and contemporary culture.

Selected Bibliography

The standard edition of *Song of Solomon* and the one used by the contributors to this volume is the New American Library paperback, issued in 1977. That edition is complete, correct, and readily available. Readers who wish to learn more about *Song of Solomon* and Morrison's other works should consult studies in the following selected bibliography.

Awkward, Michael. *Inspiriting Influences: Tradition, Revision, and Afro-American Women's Novels.* New York: Columbia University Press, 1989.

Benston, Kimberly W. "Re-weaving the 'Ulysses Scene': Enchantment, Post-Oedipal Identity, and the Buried Text of Blackness in Toni Morrison's *Song of Solomon.*" In *Comparative American Identities: Race, Sex, and Nationality in the Modern Text,* ed. Hortense J. Spillers. New York: Routledge, 1991.

Bischoff, Joan. "The Novels of Toni Morrison: Studies in Thwarted Sensitivity." *Studies in Black Literature* 6 (1976): 21–3.

Blake, Susan L. "Folklore and Community in *Song of Solomon.*" *MELUS* 7 (Fall 1980): 77–82.

Braxton, Joanne M., and Andree Nicola McLaughlin, eds. *Wild Women in the Whirlwind: Afra-American Culture and the Contemporary Literary Renaissance.* New Brunswick, NJ: Rutgers University Press, 1990.

Butler-Evans, Elliott. *Race, Gender, and Desire: Narrative Strategies in the Fiction of Toni Cade Bambara, Toni Morrison, and Alice Walker.* Philadelphia: Temple University Press, 1989.

Byerman, Keith E. *Fingering the Jagged Grain: Tradition and Form in Recent Black Fiction.* Athens: University of Georgia Press, 1985.

Campbell, Jane. *Mythic Black Fiction: The Transformation of History.* Knoxville: University of Tennessee Press, 1986.

Christian, Barbara. *Black Women Novelists: The Development of a Tradition, 1892–1976.* Westport, Conn.: Greenwood Press, 1980.

Dixon, Melvin. *Ride Out the Wilderness: Geography and Identity in Afro-American Literature.* Urbana: University of Illinois Press, 1987.

Selected Bibliography

Evans, Mari, ed. *Black Women Writers (1950–1980): A Critical Evaluation.* New York: Doubleday, Anchor Books, 1984.

Guerrero, Edward. "Tracking 'The Look' in the Novels of Toni Morrison." *Black American Literature Forum* 24 (Winter 1990): 761–73.

Harris, Trudier. *Fiction and Folklore: The Novels of Toni Morrison.* Knoxville: University of Tennessee Press, 1991.

Hirsch, Marianne. *The Mother/Daughter Plot: Narrative, Psychoanalysis, Feminism.* Bloomington: Indiana University Press, 1989.

Holloway, Karla, and Stephanie Dematrakopoulos. *New Dimensions of Spirituality: A Biracial and Bicultural Reading of the Novels of Toni Morrison.* Westport, Conn.: Greenwood Press, 1987.

Jones, Bessie W., and Audrey L. Vinson. *The World of Toni Morrison: Explorations in Literary Criticism.* Dubuque, Iowa: Kendall-Hunt, 1985.

Jones, Gayl. *Liberating Voices: Oral Tradition in African American Literature.* Cambridge: Harvard University Press, 1991.

Mason, Theodore O., Jr. "The Novelist as Conservator: Stories and Comprehension in Toni Morrison's *Song of Solomon.*" *Contemporary Literature* 29 (1988): 564–81.

McKay, Nellie Y., ed. *Critical Essays on Toni Morrison.* Boston: G. K. Hall, 1988.

Mobley, Marilyn Sanders. *Folk Roots and Mythic Wings in Sarah Orne Jewett and Toni Morrison: The Cultural Function of Narrative.* Baton Rouge: Louisiana State University Press, 1991.

Pryse, Marjorie, and Hortense J. Spillers, eds. *Conjuring: Black Women, Fiction, and Literary Tradition.* Bloomington: Indiana University Press, 1985.

Smith, Valerie. *Self-Discovery and Authority in Afro-American Narrative.* Cambridge: Harvard University Press, 1987.

Stepto, Robert. "'Intimate Things in Place': A Conversation with Toni Morrison." *Massachusetts Review* 18 (Autumn 1977): 473–89.

Tate, Claudia, ed. *Black Women Writers at Work.* New York: Continuum, 1983.

Walker, Melissa. *Down from the Mountaintop: Black Women's Novels in the Wake of the Civil Rights Movement, 1966–1989.* New Haven: Yale University Press, 1991.

Wilentz, Gay. "Civilizations Underneath: African Heritage as Cultural Discourse in Toni Morrison's *Song of Solomon.*" *African American Review* 26 (Spring 1992): 61–76.

Willis, Susan. *Specifying: Black Women Writing the American Experience.* Madison: University of Wisconsin Press, 1987.